The Divine Prayer Clock

Blake Penson
with Yoel Magdaleno

Published in Saskatoon, Canada by Faith4Action Media,
307-218 Heath Ave, Saskatoon, SK, Canada. S7S0A1.

Design and graphics by Blake Penson
Cover by Oscar Gato
Editing by Kathy Penson, Patricia Peters, Peter Hay
Published in Spanish under the title *El Reloj Divino De La Oración*.

 Underlined Scripture texts are for author's emphasis only.

ISBN: 978-0-9812689-0-3

For information on divine prayer clock news updates and conferences visit www.24-7prayerclock.com. For further inquiries contact divineprayerclock@gmail.com

Content

Forward

A Divine Agenda

See, darkness covers the earth and thick darkness is over the peoples, but the Lord rises upon you and his glory appears over you (Isaiah 60:2).

I believe that this passage defines in some way what God wants to do by bringing a new awakening to his people in their relationship with him. Blake, who has acquired experience as a pastor in Canada and in Latin America, knows what it will take. His conviction concerning the content of this manual came about after much time meditating on the theme of prayer in God's Word and observing the reality of the Church today. He believes that we are entering a special time in which God is revealing the biblical foundation necessary to confirm that prayer is meant to be continual. He does not believe that it is to be continual in a mere figurative sense, but in accordance with a divine time schedule or clock. He also believes that the Bible teaches us that each block of time in the "divine prayer clock" has specific motives of prayer.

Today we can see that the occult attaches specific spiritual significance to different times in which they carry out their dark practices. It is clear from the Scriptures that it is Satan's strategy to imitate and twist biblical truths to deceive. We should not be surprised that he has taken truths concerning a divine prayer clock, twisted them and used them for his dark plans to deceive humanity. But now, God has put into your hands the fruit of a long study by this servant of God so you can redeem the time. You no longer have to feel disoriented in your understanding and desire to fulfill God's command to pray without ceasing (1 Thessalonians 5:17). For that reason, we can affirm that this manual is more than just additional information on prayer. Rather, it is a powerful tool that will motivate you, and to which you will often refer in your life of prayer.

The Divine Prayer Clock was birthed in a time in which Blake and I were meditating together about the awakening in prayer that is taking place as a result of 24-hour prayer networks that are growing around the world. Blake and I attended a conference about a 24-hour prayer network in which the conference speaker encouraged us to pray for the nations at noon each day. I then raised these questions: Why pray at noon? And why the specific prayer motive of the nations? Does the Bible give us instructions concerning praying for the nations at noon? Blake pointed me to the answer in the book of Acts which you will also discover in this manual. However, we then asked ourselves: "If in some way the Bible teaches this, might there also be instructions or teaching that would guide us in terms of praying and interceding throughout the rest of the day?" It was a very good question that sparked considerable excitement in our hearts. If in reality there exists a biblical base for a divine prayer clock, with times and themes established by God, you can imagine the excitement and motivation for calling and organizing God's people for prayer. And so began the biblical search as Blake and I examined the Scriptures together. Although we didn't find all the answers that first day, the Lord directed us to precious passages that are in this manual. Blake continued on and has accumulated the fruit of that search in the gift that you now have in your hands.

This is, without doubt, a manual that every soldier of Christ will want to have in their possession if he or she desires to take seriously the call to pray without ceasing. God is not only waiting for us to pray, but also desires that we would be constant in our prayer life (Luke 18:1). Only in this way will we participate in the new revival that God is bringing to his people through which he will awaken the nations (Isaiah 60:1-3).

I thank God that the Divine Prayer Clock vision has been openly embraced by the Cuban Christians. They have seen that this vision is timely to refocus and renew the people of God in this nation. At the time of this printing, more than 1400 pastors and leaders have received the training through conferences and prayer retreats. And the vision continues to gain momentum across the country. Transdenominational prayer networks have sprung into existence in the communities where the teaching has been given. It is now beginning to be used as foundational teaching for church planting movements. How can we not be excited about seeing pastors and leaders from more than 30 denominations coming together to pray for the nation and seek a common vision?

Yoel Magdaleno Morales, Pastor, Cuba.
July, 2010.

Introduction

A Powerful Spiritual Weapon

The night before I was to teach what you are about to read, in a four day prayer retreat for pastors and leaders, I found myself under considerable spiritual attack in the early morning hours. I was sleeping in a room that I had reserved at a bed and breakfast in the city of Santa Clara, Cuba, close to the retreat center. Prior to falling asleep, I felt uneasy about two identical pictures that were hanging on the walls of the room. My subsequent sleep was fitful, as I came under an assault of demons in my dreams. When I awakened, I paid careful attention to the pictures. Each had what looked like an ancient clock, with the hands set at three o'clock in the morning. There was also a sun, not a brilliant, shiny sun, but a dark and oppressive one. In the picture I saw ancient lettering, which I could not distinguish. Not too long after I awakened, my friend Javier was knocking at the door. I mentioned to him the early morning attacks and the pictures. He looked at the pictures and quickly identified the dark sun as the ancient Egyptian sun god Ra and the letters as ancient Egyptian hieroglyphics. However, he did not understand the significance of the clock or the hands pointing to three o'clock in the morning. I decided to avoid further hindrance to my sleep and took the pictures off the walls and prayed against them in the name of Jesus, binding any spiritual significance they might have had.

That morning, as I prayed seeking discernment about the pictures, the Holy Spirit reminded me of a passage in the book of Exodus, when Moses led the Israelite people out of bondage in Egypt. Moses and the nation were pinned against the Red Sea by the Egyptian army led by Pharaoh. There seemed to be no way out.

So Moses began to pray and, commanded by God, lifted his staff, stretching it out over the waters of the Red Sea. The Lord separated the waters so that the Israelites could go across on dry land. Then the Egyptian army pursued them until their chariots reached the half-way point.

It was at that point that the text caught my attention.

> *During the last watch of the night the Lord looked down from the pillar of fire and cloud at the Egyptian army and threw it into confusion. He made the wheels of their chariots come off so that they had difficulty driving. And the Egyptians said: "Let's get away from the Israelites! The Lord is fighting for them against Egypt" (Exodus 14:24, 25).*

The "last watch of the night," that the text refers to, began at approximately 3 a.m. and ended at 6 a.m. or sunrise. Pharaoh, who was convinced that he was the sun god "Ra" incarnate, believed that each night Ra went through a 12-hour reincarnation and rebirth as the eternal sun god. He believed that Ra died each midnight, only to be conceived in the early morning hours, with renewed life and energy for rebirth at dawn.[1] Thus, he quickly shook off the plague of death that took all the firstborn of Egypt, including his own son. He gathered his armies for the rebirth of Ra during the last watch as a demonstration that Ra reigned supreme over the Hebrew God.

The pictures of the ancient clock on my wall were meant to communicate the supremacy of the

---

1 Erik Hornung and David Lorton, *The Ancient Books of the Afterlife* (Ithaca, NY: Cornell University Press, 1999), pp. 33-34, 36-41.

Egyptian god to those who practise the occult today. They were intended for those who believe that the ancient Egyptian religious teachings form the basis for the various streams of modern occult practices.[2] A modern witchcraft and neo-pagan religion called Wicca worships a horned god who they also call the sun god.[3] The young people that are attracted to this cult and the many around the world who seek guidance through astrology are being directed by a spiritual astral clock similar to that used by the Egyptians.[4] The message of these spiritual astral clocks is one of defiance against the Creator God Yahweh.

However, at dawn, just when Pharaoh assumed that his power as the sun god Ra would be emerging, Moses extended his rod once again in intercession. The sea closed in on the Egyptian army and destroyed it, to the last soldier.

> *Moses stretched out his hand over the sea, <u>and at daybreak</u> the sea went back to its place. The Egyptians were fleeing toward it, and the Lord swept them into the sea. The water flowed back and covered the chariots and the horsemen – the entire army of Pharaoh that had followed the Israelites into the sea. Not one of them survived (Exodus 14:27-28).*

God made clear to Israel, to Pharaoh, and to the nations

---

2 Dan Burton and David Grandy, "Egyptians and the Occult" in *Magic, Mystery and Science: The Occult In The Western Civilization* (Bloomington, Indiana: Indiana University Press, 2004), pp. 8-34

3 www.en.wikipedia.org/wiki/horned_god (accessed 2 May, 2009).

4 Mary Kay Simms, *A Time for Magick: Planetary Hours for Meditation, Rituals and Spells* (St Paul, MN: Llewellyn Worldwide, 2001), p. 13.

that it was he who ruled. He did it through the faith and intercession of one man who understood the significance of the time of God's answer and recorded it so that believers throughout the centuries would take note. You can imagine my rejoicing as the Holy Spirit answered my prayer and revealed this to me.

A few months later, I was surfing the web concerning the "3 a.m." or "last watch" theme, and I happened upon a religious internet site. On the site was a page for question and response by its inquirers from around the world. One of the themes was a cry for help for people struggling with 3 a.m. "dark experiences". The responses began as a young man named Matthew wrote:

> Sometimes I have strange experiences at night. They aren't so much nightmares but experiences with a kind of darkness....Without going into details, they seem to almost always happen around 3 a.m....I heard once that this is a somewhat well-known time for this kind of thing to happen. Does anyone have any more info?[5]

A man named Bob from Australia responded:

> I talked with Fr. Ross after Mass today, and I was the latest in a list of parishioners to express this concern to him in the past week, almost as if it's going around like the flu. And you guessed it, it all began shortly after 3 a.m. and hit its height about 30 minutes before morning light. [6]

Unfortunately, none of the responses had any real an-

5 www.catholic-pages.com (accessed 24 September, 2008).

6 Ibid.

swers for Matthew. Most of the responses were similar to Bob's as he advised:

> I think your experience is probably a demonic visit. I wouldn't worry too much about it – I mean they've got to have their entertainment I suppose...I'd ignore it if I were you...You might be a bit more spiritually sensitive than most. [7]

Satan is deceiving many concerning his power through the false teaching of a spiritual astral clock,[8] and the occult's claims of authority and control in the "witching hours".[9] It is time for the "Moses" of our day to extend the rod of intercession in Christ's name. The rod that God has placed in our hands is prayer that is strategic, with an understanding of the times and motives established by him. After discovering these exciting truths in Exodus, both Javier and I decided to get up early the next morning and pray during the last watch (3 a.m. to 6 a.m.). We prayed for the prayer retreat and also for the family that owned the bed and breakfast where we were staying. The owner of the house listened wide-eyed as we shared the deception behind the pictures that had been on the walls of my room. She then chose to dispose of them and asked to hear more about Jesus Christ and about prayer. After hearing about the authority and power of Jesus, the owner´s daughter-in-law decided to put her trust in Jesus Christ, and prayed with us. During the prayer retreat, others decided to get up and take turns praying the night watches. It was exciting to hear the stories of how God manifested him-

---

7 Ibid.

8 Mary Kay Simms, p. 13.

9 "Witching Hour", Wikipedia, http://www.en.wikipedia.org/wiki/witching_hour (accessed 25 September, 2008).

self to them as well.

It is not my intent in this introduction to emphasize any one prayer watch of the prayer clock over any other watch. Instead, it is my desire to awaken believers to their authority in Christ to extend the influence and power of his kingdom through prayer and intercession. As the movement of the 24-hour prayer networks continues to extend around the world, the understanding and practice of the divine prayer clock could become an essential component for its momentum and impact.

I. The House Of Prayer

Throughout the Gospels, Christ made it clear that his concept of spiritual accomplishment was much different than the religious leaders of his day, or for that matter of our day. Christ did not come to inspire the construction of church buildings. In fact, he declared the end to any plan focused on construction as its measure of success when he prophesied the destruction of the temple of Herod(Matthew 24:1, 2). In his declaration, he confirmed that his purpose in coming was to raise up a spiritual temple of prayer for all nations, through his body (John 2:19-21; Mark 11:17). The bricks would not be of mortar or cement but of living stones. They would be people born and made alive by the living Spirit of God through faith in Christ through prayer (1 Peter 2:4, 5). If the plan to establish a church is focused on the construction of a building, then it is merely a copy of Herod's blueprint and is doomed to spiritual failure. But if our plan is to raise up a church through prayer, discipling people to have an ongoing living encounter with Christ through being in constant communication with him, we have Jesus' blueprint. And his blueprint is guaranteed to be approved by heaven's building inspector.

When Christ comes to gather his church he will be coming for a spiritual temple of living stones, all in constant prayer. He will not be coming for an organization busily planning new building or expansion projects.

Jesus' words were the following:

> *And will not God bring about justice for his chosen ones, who cry out to him day and night? Will he keep putting them off? I tell you, he will see that they get justice, and quickly. However, when the Son of Man comes will he find faith on the earth? (Luke 18:7,8).*

When Jesus speaks of faith in this passage, he is speaking about persevering prayer. The introduction of the parable confirms Jesus´ lesson that true faith manifests itself in constant, persistent prayer. *"Then Jesus told his disciples a parable to show them that they should always pray and not give up" (Luke 18:1).* In other words, for Jesus, true faith and ongoing persistent prayer are one and the same. The Apostle Paul declares that the goal of all ministry, even evangelism and the preaching of the Word, is to bring people to the point where they will begin to exercise faith by praying and calling on the name of Jesus (Romans 10:13,14). Faith without prayer is not genuine faith. When Christ comes to gather his church, he will be coming for a spiritual temple of living stones, all in constant persevering prayer. He will not be coming for an organization busily planning new building or expansion projects. One day he will prove our work with divine fire, whatever that work may be (1 Corinthians 3:13-15). The cement blocks, wood and tile will not remain (2 Peter 3:11-13). The living stones will.

If the Lord has blessed you with a beautiful structure in which to meet together, be humbly thankful. But, remember that your building was not what motivated him to die on the cross. That was not the house that God wanted and has been waiting for. The house that God wants was prophesied almost 3000 years ago and its design and architecture cannot be accomplished with the means and resources of typical construction. However, the great news is that God revealed in his Word the blueprint, the methods and the resources so that we would be participants in Christ's work to build the house that God desires.

Questions For Reflection:

1. How do you think the members of your local church would define "the house of God"?

2. Is there a disparity between the current concept of the house of God and that of our Lord Jesus Christ in the Scriptures (Mark 11: 17)? If so, why the difference?

3. Make a list of the present programs and activities that represent the life and attendance of your local church. On a priority scale of 1 to 10, where would you place prayer among the other programs and activities?

4. The early church took measures to ensure that the priority of prayer and the teaching of the Word were not displaced (Acts 6:1-7). What measures might your local church take to restore prayer to its rightful place in the spiritual life of its members?

II. The Tabernacle of David

One of the most important prophecies concerning the house that God wants is found in Acts 15:16-18 where the writer quotes Amos 9:11-12.[10]

> *After this I will return and rebuild David's fallen tent. Its ruins I will rebuild, and I will restore it, that the remnant of men may seek the Lord, and all the Gentiles who bear my name, says the Lord, who does these things that have been known for ages.*

The "remnant of men" – your neighborhood, municipality, city and nation – will turn to Christ as a result of the tabernacle of David being rebuilt. If revival in your community, your nation, and around the world is contingent upon this prophecy, then it is critical that we understand it, as quoted and interpreted by its speaker in the book of Acts.

The palace from which Christ governs is the house of prayer. First his kingdom will be established in the hearts of men, and then the governments of this world will be replaced by his government.

At the Jerusalem council, James was seeking Scriptural evidence that would support the spiritual redefinition of the house of God as Paul was redefining it (Ephesians 2:19-22). The physical temple in Jerusalem,

---

10 Graham Truscott, *The Power Of His Presence* (Burbank, California: World Map Press, 1969), pp. 4, 5.

with the Mosaic ceremonial law, was still vibrant and active at the time of Paul's teaching. However, as Paul was reaching the Gentiles for Christ, he was also giving new meaning to the house of God. He redefined it as a spiritual house or temple in Christ, in which the building materials were the people who believed in Christ, Jew and Gentile alike.

> *In him the whole building is joined together and rises to become a holy temple in the Lord. And in him you too are being built together to become a dwelling in which God lives by his Spirit (Ephesians 2:21, 22).*

There was opposition to this spiritual redefinition, not only from the Jewish religious leaders, but also from the Jewish Christian community in Jerusalem, until James prophetically spoke of the tabernacle of David.

The tabernacle of David was a tent in which David accommodated the ark of God's presence when he brought it to Jerusalem (1 Chronicles 16:1; 2 Samuel 6:17). The astonishing thing is that the tabernacle of Moses was still in existence at that time and was located in Gibeon (1 Chronicles 16:39). The tabernacle of Moses had been without the ark of God's presence for almost 100 years (during the lifetime of Samuel, Saul, and part of David's reign). It had been captured by the Philistines in a battle that devastated Israel as a consequence of the sin of their religious leaders (1 Samuel 3, 4). It was then returned to them when God punished the Philistine nation with plagues of tumors (1 Samuel 5, 6). The Israelites left the ark in the countryside, unsure of their relationship with God - until David became king. David yearned for God's presence to be with the nation once again. Surprisingly, rather than returning the ark of God's presence to the Most Holy Place in the tabernacle of Moses in Gibeon, David put it in a simple tent at Jerusalem. It was a historic and prophetic moment of redefinition and shift. And God did not punish David for leaving the Most Holy Place vacant in Moses' tabernacle. The ark remained in the simple tabernacle of David until David's son, Solomon, built an elaborate temple many years later. However, note that the prophecy mentioned in Amos and Acts makes no mention of the temple of Solomon or of the tabernacle of Moses, but only of the tabernacle of David.

What fascinates me is that the tabernacle of David was a simple tent without blocks or walls of any type. It did not even have a curtain separating the Holy Place from the Most Holy Place. There appeared to be open access to the ark of God's presence as for the first time the regular Levites were permitted to minister freely before the ark along with the priests (1 Chronicles 16:4, 6). Another interesting element that distinguishes David's tabernacle was the nonstop ministry of prayer and worship before the ark (1 Chronicles 16:4, 37). David later organized ongoing prayer and praise through creating a system of 24 prayer and praise shifts (1 Chronicles 24).[11] It is this simple tabernacle, a tabernacle of historic and prophetic shift, that James refers to in Acts 15. It was a tabernacle of open access for all God's servants, with ongoing prayer and praise. It is this simple tabernacle of David that was to explain Paul's redefinition of the house of God as a spiritual house and as the key for world revival.

In the prophecy, James cites the rebuilding of the ruins of the tabernacle of David as the condition for what was taking place among the Gentile nations

---

11 Omar Oviedo and Idaly Rivera, *Un Llamado de Dios A Orar Continuamente* (Armenia, Colombia: Publicaciones Alianza, 2003), p. 26.

through Paul. In the original text in Amos, the ruins are described as having holes or broken places in the walls. However, since there were no walls or physical ruins, what was James referring to in the prophecy? There can only be one explanation: the ruins are spiritual ruins of a spiritual house. What needed rebuilding was the open access for all to God's presence, with ongoing prayer and praise. There were to be no barriers or restrictions that would keep the people from communing with God at any moment around the clock. God said to David that one of his sons would build the house that God wanted, and God would confirm his throne forever (1 Chronicles 17:11-15). It was Jesus, not Solomon, who would build the house that God was waiting for. Jesus was the Son of David whose throne would be confirmed forever. He was the one to fulfill the prophecy of Amos.

The rebuilding of the tabernacle of David was the re-establishment of God's rule on earth through David's family line in Christ, through a house of continuous prayer and worship. His throne would not be re-established through political or military means, but through spiritual means. And he would rebuild the fallen tabernacle of David, not with stone blocks but with living stones. It is through this house that his kingdom is to be established forever.

The palace from which Christ governs and will govern is the house of prayer. First his kingdom will be established in the hearts of men (Luke 17:21) and then the governments of this world will be replaced by his government (Revelation 11:15, Psalm 2). There will be internal order before there can be external order. And this order will be re-established through the rebuilt tabernacle of David, a spiritual house with a design of open access for all, with continuous 24/7 prayer and worship. This is the house through which Christ will extend his rule around the globe. For that reason, Jesus said: *"My house will be called a house of prayer for all nations" (Mark 11:17).*

I believe that Jesus is once again revealing his plan to his people for the rebuilt tabernacle of David. The preaching of the gospel will only have impact when the house of open access and continuous prayer is restored. Paul saw the results in his time because continuous prayer, night and day, was the spiritual house from which they ministered (1 Thessalonians 3:10, 5:17; 2 Timothy 1:3). I also believe that the rebuilding has been in process since the early church but has experienced stoppages each time the body of Christ has deviated from Christ's blueprint for his house. Jesus, as the cornerstone (Isaiah 28:16; Ephesians 2:20), has set in place the foundation and provided, in himself, all the resources necessary to unite us and raise us up as a holy spiritual temple that will fill the earth with his glory. But it is our responsibility, as living stones, to be built into the cornerstone of Christ through faith expressed in ongoing prayer and worship. In reality, the house of God is the only house that is a living organism, in which the living stones mutually build each other up through their relationship and communion with the Living Stone, Jesus Christ (1 Peter 2:4-6).

The religious leaders and people during Jesus´ earthly life disqualified themselves as builders of God´s true house (Acts 4:11). We too need to be careful. The Lord is the master builder and we are the workers. Unless we build according to his design and direction our efforts will be in vain. *"Unless the Lord builds the house, its builders labor in vain" (Psalm 127:1).* Being religiously active does not qualify one to be a builder of the true house of God. To qualify one must have an intimate relationship with the Lord through a true faith that is manifested in prayer. The plans, structures and religious traditions of men have often hindered ongoing access to God's presence. Like the tabernacle or temple without the ark, we can be so easily deceived into thinking that religious form and tradition are acceptable. We can become satisfied with the trappings and forget that the essence of our faith is intimacy with God through prayer.

In North America, we wonder why we do not see God´s supernatural moving in our churches and in our communities. North American pastors pray an average of 22 minutes a day. This compares to Chinese pastors who pray an average of two hours and Korean pastors, like Yongii Cho, who pray three to five hours a day.[12] A friend of mine attended a pastors' conference in which there were Korean pastors present. My friend overheard a North American pastor laughing as he ridiculed the Korean pastors for having no time for anything else but prayer. Is it any wonder that the Korean church has grown so significantly in the last 30 years and that the nation has been so blessed? It's time to take an honest look at our relationship with God as individuals and as a local church.

This book is really evidence of God's mercy in my life, rather than proof of persistent intimacy with God. Only two years previous to the writing of this book, my life was quickly losing all signs of spiritual vitality. I had been deceived into thinking that working for God could replace intimacy with God. It was by means of a dream given to a new believer (for whom I was supposed to be a spiritual example) that God restored me to an intimate relationship with himself. My friend described the odd dream to me in an email, thinking it was for himself. He

---

12 Stuart Robinson, "Praying- The Price of Revival," www.globalchristians.org/articles/payprice.htm (accessed 30 Sept, 2008).

asked me to seek God for interpretation of the dream. In the first part of the dream, he saw a house in a terrible state of disrepair. There were holes in the roof and walls. Many years had passed since it had been repaired or maintained. It looked like an abandoned home. In the second part of the dream, there were two birds. One bird was pecking out the eyes of the other bird, but the bird being attacked passively allowed the first bird to blind it and then kill it. With a desire to help my friend, I began to seek God concerning the dream. As I did, God revealed to me that the dream was not for my friend but for me. It was my spiritual life, God's house of prayer in me, that was in disrepair. Over time, I had simply presumed upon my relationship with God without doing anything to nurture it. Love that is not nurtured slowly dies. My carelessness concerning my times of prayer with God was killing the love and joy that he had birthed in my heart for him. It was my spiritual neglect that was represented by the attacking bird intent on destroying any signs of spiritual life and intimacy with God. I had religion but I was losing the relationship. I was working for God but I was not enjoying him. Thanks to the mercy of God through the dream he gave to my friend, the Spirit of God awakened and called me before it was too late.

It is the call to return to our first love from mere religious activity that will revolutionize the church of the last days (Revelation 2:4, 5). The rebuilding is starting once again in our time as a hunger for spiritual intimacy through prayer is growing. A movement of 24/7 interdenominational prayer networks is springing up around the globe in local churches, paving the way for the preaching of the gospel, global repentance and worldwide revival. Christ is once again unveiling his plan to his people. In the next pages of this manual you are going to see how this plan is revealed and realized in Christ, as God's people prepare and organize according to the pattern he has given us. Moses built on earth a material copy of God's design for a spiritual tabernacle (Acts 7:44). We have the incredible opportunity, under Christ's direction, to participate together in building on earth the actual spiritual house that already exists in heaven .

> *As you come to him, the living Stone – rejected by men but chosen by God and precious to him - you also, like living stones, are being built into a spiritual house to be a holy priesthood, offering spiritual sacrifices acceptable to God through Jesus Christ (1 Peter 2:5).*

You have the opportunity to be part of this historic and prophetic moment. But each one must choose whether he or she will participate. Will you be part of the greatest building project in the history of mankind?

Questions for Reflection:

1. What was the difference between the tabernacle of David and the tabernacle of Moses?

2. How did that difference become the key motivator in the ongoing growth and influence of the early church (Acts 15:16-18)?

3. For David and also for the early Church, the House of God (the House of Prayer) was the place of God´s rule on earth (Acts 4:23-31). Does the present practice of prayer reflect this biblical concept? If not, what are the reasons?

4. What can you do to help restore the conviction concerning the supreme call of prayer in your own life and in that of your local church?

III. The Origin Of Time And The Bible

Before we delve into the concept of the divine prayer clock, we must understand how the concept of time developed within the nation of Israel throughout biblical history. In reality, the Hebrews probably did not have a concept of time as refined as a 24-hour clock until the period of the Roman Empire. Before and during the era of Moses (approximately 1500 – 1400 BC), it appears that the Egyptians were developing the concept of exact time measurement. Traditionally, time was measured through studying the general movement of the sun in the day and the moon and stars at night. However, the Egyptians developed instruments to numerically measure time in an exact way, assigning 12 hours to the night, 10 hours to the day, and 2 hours to dawn and dusk, for a total of 24 hours.[13] The Egyptians used a sundial for the daylight hours.[14] They used a star chart

If we make time our god, filling our lives with more and more activities to find fulfillment, ultimately they will consume us. Life will lose its meaning and purpose.

13 Otto Neugebauer, *The Exact Sciences In Antiquity* (Dover, UK: Courier, 1969), p. 86.

14 Sarah Symons, "Shadow Clocks and Sloping Sundials of The Egyptian New Kingdom Period," British Sundial Society Bulletin, No. 98.3, Oct. 1998, pp. 30-38.

as well as a water clock for the night-time hours. [15] Archaeological discovery of these instruments has dated their use to 1500 - 1300 BC.[16]

The numerical measurement of time by the Egyptians was not merely the assignment of a numerical value to the positions of the sun and stars. The numerical measurement of time was also given a religious significance. Day and night were personified by the deity "Ra". As earlier mentioned, the 12-hour night was understood by Egyptians to be the reincarnation and rebirth of the sun god Ra. The details are found in what is called "Amduat: The Book of the Hidden Chambers". They are in the format of a series of prayers to the sun god Ra (Re).[17] They were inscribed on the walls of the tomb of Tutmosis III, Pharaoh of Egypt.[18] Tutmosis III reigned from approximately 1479 to 1426 BC.[19] He was probably the Pharaoh mentioned in the Exodus account. Calculations of the biblical date based on 1 Kings 6:1 place the exodus at approximately 1440 BC, within the timeframe of the reign of Tutmosis III.[20] Moses was raised in Pharaoh's courts and was well-versed in the Egyptian sciences and the religious teachings (Acts 7:22). Yet, it appears that Moses chose to disassociate himself from the numerical

---

15 Sarah Symons, "Two Fragments of Diagonal Star Clocks in the British Museum," JHA XIII, 2007, pp. 257-260.

16 Eric Bruton, *The History of Clocks and Watches* (London: Orbis Publishing, 1979), pp. 13, 20.

17 Hornung and Lorton, "The Amduat" in *The Ancient Books of the Afterlife* (Ithaca, New York: Cornell University Press, 1999), pp. 27 – 53.

18 Joann Fletcher and Delia Pemberton, *Treasures of the Pharaohs* (San Francisco, CA: Chronicle Books, 2004), pp. 61-62.

19 Theodore Abt and Erik Hornung, *History of Ancient Egypt* (Ithaca, New York: Cornell University Press, 1999), pp. 82-83.

20 www.en.wikipedia.org/wiki/TheExodus (accessed 14 September, 2008).

religious time sciences of Egypt in establishing the pattern for Israel to follow. God used Moses to separate the Jewish people from the Egyptian culture and sciences which were intermingled with false religious beliefs.

We discover that the Israelites were guided by their own time system based on a lunar calendar which was given to them through God's covenant. The first month was Nisan (or Abib, Exodus 12:2, 13:4), marking God's saving intervention in the Passover through the shed blood of a lamb painted on their doorposts. They were to learn about time in terms of God's saving activity. The significance of time was not to be discovered in an Egyptian god, but in the Creator God Jehovah, and in trusting and worshiping him. The days of the week were associated with the creation account in the first chapter of the Bible (Genesis 1). In contrast, the days of our week have been named to honor Roman, Norse and Germanic gods.[21] Throughout most of Old Testament Hebrew history, we do not see the Jewish people using numerical time instruments and the corresponding 12-hour day and a 12-hour night. Daily time was measured in accordance with the creation account, with the sun, moon and stars themselves seen as God's instruments of time.

> *God made two great lights – the greater light to govern the day and the lesser light to govern the night. He also made the stars. God set them in the expanse of the sky to give light on the earth, to govern the day and the night, and to separate light from darkness. And God saw that it was good. And there was evening, and there was morning – the fourth day (Genesis 1:16 – 19).*

---

21 Gerald Erichsen, "Planetary Hours of the Week," www.spanish.about.com/od/historyofspanish/a/names of day.htm. (accessed 11 May, 2009).

Moses, the writer of the Pentateuch (the first five books of the Bible), was establishing the pattern for God's covenant people, chosen by him for his times and purposes. Approximately 500 years later, as we shall see, David was still using the general movement of the celestial bodies to indicate time.

It was not only the Egyptians who played a role in developing the concept of time and the 24-hour clock that we have today. After the Egyptians, there were the Babylonians and the Greeks.[22] It appears that often the association was made between numerical time and the gods of the culture. For instance, the Greeks chose the word "chronos" to describe the concept of a measure or portion of time. [23] However, "chronos" did not merely express the concept of a unit of time, but also the idea that it could be destructive. Chronos, in Greek mythology, was a god who ate or consumed his own children.[24]The Greeks unknowingly were communicating a great truth: if we make time and activity our god, filling our lives with more and more events to find fulfillment, ultimately we will be consumed by them. Life will lose purpose and value. The worship of time and activity is doomed to be a fateful choice.

The other Greek word for time was "kairos". The essence of its use in the Greek culture was the "decisive moment" presented to one. To recognize and receive that moment was to discover one's destiny. To not recognize and miss it was to destroy one's destiny.[25] "Kairos" was a season, a unique moment in life that was

---

22 Neugebauer, p. 81.

23 Delling, "Chronos," *Theological Dictionary of The New Testament* (Logos Electronic Scholar's Library, 2007).

24 Scott Littleton, *Gods, Goddesses, and Mythology* (Terrytown, NY: Marshall Cavendish Corporation, 2005), pp. 335-336.

25 Delling, "Kairos," *TDNT.*

meant to be a gift for the purpose of redeeming time and giving it form and purpose. That is what God was trying to teach his people through the covenant time framework of months and Sabbath days pregnant with God's eternal plans and purposes.[26] They were "kairos" moments, offering the Hebrews the opportunity to embrace an eternal purpose and destiny for their lives and activity. The Sabbath day was a call to rest, remember and review the creation account, the covenant, and the reason for which people were created. Just as they were created in God's likeness and image to be a reflection of him on earth, so also their time was to be a reflection of an eternal mindset. Rather than being consumed by meaningless activity, God has called us to a place of rest where we can be restored to the eternal meaning and purpose for which we were created.

WIth sin and humanity's choice to turn its back on God's plans and purposes, our understanding of time was divorced from eternity. We were confronted with a context of time, a "chronos" that brought death. Since then our days have been filled with anxiety, rushing around in circles of mind-numbing activity to try to forget that time is running out. We have been deceived into thinking that fulfillment is found in filling life with as much activity as possible. In reality, the secret to life is rediscovering its original purpose.

The good news is that Jesus, the Alpha and Omega, has come to us. He has come within the "chronos" of our daily lives and schedules. He did not come to consume us, but rather to sacrifice himself for us, and restore God's divine and eternal purposes in us. The Lord of the Sabbath has come to remind us of the place of divine rest in our lives. He calls us to rest in him so that he may reveal to us his purpose for life. It is a "kai-

---

26 Mark Buchanan, *The Rest of God* (Nashville, Tennessee: Thomas Nelson, 2006), p. 36.

ros" time, a time of destiny. We must choose to embrace our destiny or lose it.

Jerusalem did not recognize its destiny moment, its "kairos," when it came to them. *"They will not leave one stone on another, because you did not recognize the time of God's coming to you" (Luke 19:44)*. It is important to note Jesus' prophetic words in response to his people's choice to not recognize and receive their divine "kairos" moment. Jerusalem would be destroyed and, as Matthew relates, their temple would also be destroyed (Matthew 24: 1, 2). The divine plans and purposes for the lives of God's people are intricately connected with God's house – the house of prayer. Jesus, the "kairos" of God, has come to redeem our daily lives, our "chronos", with divine purpose and meaning. If we choose to recognize and receive this "kairos" moment, it can only be done by expressing our faith and resting in him through prayer. Being with Jesus through prayer must become the priority of our daily "chronos" schedules if it is to be redeemed with heaven's divine "kairos".

What you are about to read in the rest of this manual will stir and challenge you as you come to realize how God has invaded our "chronos" time schedules with his divine "kairos" clock. I call it the divine prayer clock. The Scriptures give details of how God's "kairos" clock was initially developed through David and then received its fullest significance in the life and work of the Son of David, Jesus Christ. It is this clock that reveals to us the blueprints for building the house that God wants. That is the task for which you were created. It is your eternal destiny. Jesus is offering you and me a divine opportunity to do the works which were designed for us from before time (Ephesians 2:10, 22). Will you recognize and receive this "kairos" moment? Will you be part of the rebuilding of the fallen tabernacle of David? If so, read on.

Questions for Reflection:

1. Do you perceive yourself as a person controlled by time and circumstances or as a believer in Christ who can influence the times and situations around you (see Joshua 10:12, 13)? Explain.

2. Are your day´s activities inspired by your prayers or are your prayers a reaction to your day´s activity (see Mark 1:35-39)? Why do you think that is your spiritual reality?

3. How can we be changed from being "chronos" focused to "kairos" focused in our lifestyle (Acts 17: 26 - 28; Psalm 91:12; Revelation 1:8)?

IV. Time In The Prayers Of David

During the reign of King David, time was marked during the day by the position of the sun: "boqer"[27] – sunrise, "tsohar"[28] – midday, and "ereb"[29] – sunset. God used David to reveal the house of God as a spiritual house of continual prayer, with specific times of prayer. He prayed at each of the three daytime positions of the sun. *"Evening, morning, and noon I cry out in distress, and he hears my voice" (Psalm 55:17).*

We need to change our paradigm for structuring our days from an activity-based rhythm to a spiritually-based rhythm.

In David's lifetime, the night was divided into three night watches. The watches of the night were determined by the position of the celestial bodies. The watches began with "nessheph" – twilight (2 Kings 7:5),[30] continued with "chatsowth" – midnight (Psalm 119:62),[31] and the last watch came to an end with "boqer"- sunrise (Psalm 46:5). David affirmed his faithfulness to pray the watches of the night. *"My eyes stay open through the watches of the night that I may meditate on your promises" (Psalm 119:148).* Da-

---

27 J. Strong, "boqer," (Strong's Hebrew #1242), *Strong's Exhaustive Concordance Of The Bible* (Logos Electronic Scholar's Library, 2007).

28 J. Strong, "tsohar," (Strong's Hebrew #6672).

29 J. Strong, "ereb," (Strong's Hebrew # 6153).

30 J. Strong, "nessheph," (Strong's Hebrew #5399).

31 J. Strong, "chatsowth," (Strong's Hebrew #2676).

vid also declared: *"At midnight I rise to give you thanks for your righteous laws" (Psalm 119:62).* In Psalm 63:1 he says: *"O God, thou art my God; early will I seek thee"* (KJV). It appears that David did not miss any of the watches of the night for being in communion with his God. *"On my bed I remember you; I think of you through the watches of the night" (Psalm 63:6).* As a shepherd, David learned to sleep lightly at night while caring for his sheep. This vigilance prepared him for the great call that he would receive from God. As the shepherd king over Israel, David would get up to pray at the start of each watch. His passion was to commune with God continually through observing a system of prayer watches. But David's passion for God's presence did not end with the three positions of the sun and the three watches of the night. In addition to those six times, David found a seventh moment in the day to seek God's presence. *"Seven times a day I praise you for your righteous laws" (Psalm 119:164).* We do not know whether David took fifteen minutes, a half hour, an hour or more in each of these times of devotion to God. In reality, he did not have the means to measure time precisely as we do today. What we do know is that David connected in a meaningful way with God throughout the day and night. His life was an ongoing conversation and communion with him. That is the secret to understanding the prayer clock. It is developing the habit of connecting with God regularly throughout the day and night.

This is quite incredible when one considers the tremendous responsibility that David had as king, being both the civil and military leader. He could have easily allowed his daily schedule to be dominated by pressing and urgent responsibilities. But David had a spiritually-based rhythm to life, rather than an activity-based rhythm. His activity was informed and directed by his communion with God. David came to the conclusion that his civil and military responsibilities should be regulated by his prayer structure. David could have tried to convince himself and everyone else of his importance through an agenda filled with activity, without time for God or anyone else. But, he wanted it to be evident that the source of his authority, wisdom, wealth and might was God. He wanted everyone to know that, ultimately, it was God who was King.

If we are to be part of God's plan to rebuild the tabernacle of David to bring about worldwide revival, we must pay attention to the example of David. We need to change the paradigm for structuring our days from an activity-based rhythm to a spiritually-based rhythm of life. We also need to think about how we can organize ourselves corporately to fulfill the amazing prophecy concerning David's tabernacle. If David recognized the importance of organizing the Levites and the people to ensure continuous prayer and worship, it should move us to do the same to rebuild the tabernacle of David in our day. David knew that if the nation of Israel was to follow God and experience his blessing, then his prayers alone would not be sufficient. Not many of us will be able to sustain a prayer schedule like David's to pray during the day and at every watch of the night. I believe God gave David an extra measure of grace as the founder of this tabernacle. We can organize ourselves as a church to cover all of the hours of prayer and ensure that at least one of us is before God in prayer at all times. Hopefully, everyone will be motivated to become involved by participating in at least one of the watches of the night or hours of prayer during the day.

Questions for Reflection:

1. If you have had or now have a scheduled prayer plan, explain your schedule and your reasons for that schedule. Has it worked well for you? Why or why not?

2. Rather than adding prayer to his daily agenda, King David organized his agenda around prayer. What is your initial reaction to such a lifestyle? Why?

3. David also organized the Levites and his people around a 24/7 spiritual lifestyle and agenda through the tabernacle of David. What might be some of the obstacles in rebuilding the tabernacle of David through a 24/7 prayer plan in your local church?

4. How might those obstacles be overcome?

V. Time In The Prayers Of The New Testament

The New Testament Clock

The concept of time during David's reign continued the tradition inherited from Moses. The days were marked by the position of the sun (2 Kings 20:10,11). The watches of the night were determined by the position of the celestial bodies. As explained previously, it is likely that Moses chose to reject the further division of time into hours for spiritual reasons. Thus, the concept of the day divided into numerical units of time does not reappear until the Babylonian period (2 Kings 20:9-11), and it is openly accepted in the New Testament Scriptures during the Roman period. By the era of the Roman civilization, numerical time measurement appeared to have more of a military than a religious connotation. The concept of the 12-hour day and 12-hour night accompanied the Roman legions as they extended the empire. Trumpet calls sounded by Roman soldiers marked the changing of the night watches every three hours.[32] The marking of time was a sign of Roman

Following the disciples' example, we too can learn to make time with Jesus the priority of our daily schedule.

32 Sarah Elise Phang, *Roman Military Service* (Cambridge, England: Cambridge University Press, 2008), p. 213.

presence and sovereignty. The change to a military emphasis is significant because God was about to invade time and space in the person of the Alpha and Omega, Jesus Christ.

Time, in the Roman day, was marked by 12-hour sundials and at night by water clocks that were much more refined than those of the Egyptians. The 12 hours of the day and the 12 hours of the night were grouped further into 3 hour blocks.[33] This explains the difference between the non-numerical prayer clock of David in the Old Testament and the terminology used in the numerical time clock of the Gospels. For example, Jesus says in John's Gospel: *"Are there not twelve hours of daylight?" (John 11:9).* Rather than describing time solely by the positions of the sun, a numerical time designation was given. The forum bell rang in the cities of the Roman Empire to mark the beginning of the day (6 a.m. our time).[34] The next bell marked mid-morning (9 a.m. our time) and was called the third hour (Acts 2:15), as three hours had passed since sunrise. The midday bell (12 noon) was called the sixth hour (Acts 10:9), and marked the beginning of lunch break. The mid-afternoon bell (3 p.m. our time) was called the ninth hour (Acts 3:1), and was a call back to work.[35] The 3-hour blocks of time were also further divided. Four p.m. our time would have been the tenth hour. In the Gospel of John, the writer makes a comment about two of Jesus' followers in relation to the tenth hour. They had decided to stay with him because it was late and darkness was fast approaching. *"So they went and saw where he was staying, and spent that day with him. It was about the tenth hour" (John 1:39b).* Following the disciples' example, we too

---

33 Ibid.

34 Phyllis Tickle, *The Divine Hours* (New York: Double Day, 2000), p. x.

35 Phyllis Tickle, p. x.

can learn to make time with Jesus the priority of our daily schedule.

The hours of the night were also designated numerically (Acts 23:23). Generally, the 3-hour blocks of time during the night were called "watches", as a reflection of the roman military system of observance and control. As mentioned, the signal for the end of one watch and the start of the next was a trumpet blast, not a bell as during the day. The first watch began at 6 p.m. our time. The second watch started at 9 p.m. The third watch began at midnight, with the final watch beginning at 3 a.m. and ending at 6 a.m. Jesus referred to the watches in terms of spiritual vigilance. He describes the four night watches in the Gospel of Mark (13:35 – 37).

In the following pages you will learn the prayer times established in the New Testament in what I call the divine prayer clock. In this prayer clock, you will discover a biblical prayer plan that will transform your concept of time and your daily schedule. You will see how God wants to infuse your daily agenda with divine purpose and power in the person and work of his Son, Jesus Christ.

Questions for Reflection:

1. What are the New Testament (Roman equivalent) times for 6 a.m., 9 a.m., 12 noon, and 3 p.m.?

2. What are the New Testament (Roman equivalent) times for the 6 p.m., 9 p.m., 12 midnight, and 3 a.m. prayer times?

3. Why do we find it important to schedule our daily activities according to specific times?

4. Why do you think it might be important to remember the biblical prayer clock?

The Hour Of Incense (6 a.m.)

The first 3-hour prayer block was known by the term: "The Hour of Incense." It began with the sun's rising and, in reality, had been established from the time of Moses. *"Aaron must burn fragrant incense on the altar every morning when he tends the lamps" (Exodus 30:7,8)*. After being up all night to ensure that the lamp did not go out, the priest finally snuffed out the flame at sunrise. He then went before God, wearing the breastpiece and the ephod to intercede for the people (Exodus 28:4). It was a practice that continued right up to the time of the Gospels, when we discover Zechariah interceding before God while the people prayed and waited outside (Luke 1:9-12). *"And when the time for the burning of incense came, all the assembled worshipers were praying outside" (Luke 1:10).*

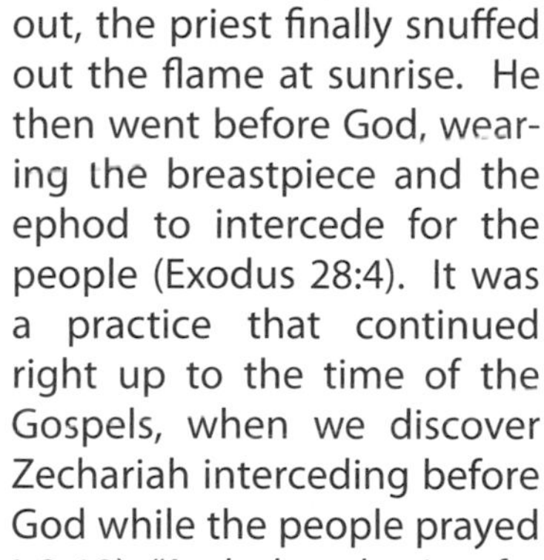

It is the fragrance of our prayers at dawn, our communion with God, which is the fragrant garden In which he loves to walk in the morning.

It was the hour when God promised to meet with his people and speak to them, if they would come in the prescribed way at the prescribed time.

> *"This is what you are to offer on the altar regularly each day: two lambs a year old. Offer one in the morning and the other at twilight....For the generations to come this burnt offering is to be made regularly at the entrance to the Tent of Meeting before the Lord. There I will meet you and speak to you; there also I will meet with the Israelites, and the place will*

> *be consecrated by my glory....Then I will dwell among the Israelites and be their God " (Exodus 29: 38, 39, 42, 43,45).*

The very first call to prayer each day reminds us of the incredible opportunity to come in Christ, the Lamb of God, and meet with God to hear his voice. The focus of all prayer is to meet with God. It is the divine meeting place. The priority of prayer is to first hear God and listen to him. Kneel before him with the Scriptures opened in anticipation that he will speak to you and write on the tablet of your heart. It is there that we come to know God, and where he works in us to have the will to act according to his good purposes (Philippians 2:13). Obedience and holiness are never experienced separate from God's presence and Word working in us through prayer.

The Hour of Incense has even more to teach us. Two very important symbols of this prayer time were the incense and the precious stones on the priest's breastpiece. The incense represented the prayers of God's people. *"...Each one had a harp and they were holding golden bowls full of incense, which are the prayers of the saints" (Revelation 5:8).* Take note of the harps as well. This prayer was not merely praying lists as we often do today. These were prayers founded in worship, magnifying the person and character of God as they prayed and interceded. This is the model of prayer that not only David but also the prophet Elisha left for us (2 Kings 3:15). It is the type of prayer that moves the heart of God, or should I say the nose of God. The fact that God links the symbol of incense to prayer indicates that God has a spiritual sense of smell that is as real as our physical sense of smell. It is our prayers, if truly offered with sincerity, that delight him even more than the fragrance of a rose. It is the fragrance of our prayers at dawn, our communion with God, which is the fragrant garden in which he loves to walk in the morning.

In the book of Revelation, we find some verses that are in one way disturbing and at the same time encouraging with respect to the prayers of the church in the last days.

> *Another angel, who had a golden censer, came and stood at the altar. He was given much incense to offer, with the prayers of all the saints, on the golden altar before the throne. The smoke of the incense, together with the prayers of the saints, went up before God from the angel's hand (Revelation 8:3,4).*

The disturbing part is that the angel needed to be given much more incense to add to the prayers of the saints. It appears that the prayers of the saints were insufficient for God to move on the earth. The ministry of prayer has been almost forgotten in the church today. It is time to light the altar of our hearts and burn the incense of our prayers. The encouraging part of these verses is that God appears to be ready to add whatever is lacking in our prayers if we would only be willing to pray.

Another important symbol of this first call to prayer was the breastpiece with the precious stones. There were twelve precious stones, each stone representing one of the twelve tribes of Israel (Exodus 28:21, 29). It was a divine reminder for the priest to intercede for the people in the way that God saw them.

> *"You yourselves have seen what I did to Egypt, and how I carried you on eagles' wings and brought you to myself. Now if you obey me fully and keep my covenant, then out of all nations you will be my treasured possession. Although the whole earth is mine, you will be for me a kingdom of priests and a holy nation" (Exodus 19:4-6).*

We are to intercede for our brothers and sisters remembering how God sees them. We are of such incredible value to God that he calls us his treasured possession, and gave his Son as a ransom for us (1 Timothy 2:6). As we awaken in the morning to pray, we need to remind ourselves of how God sees us as his children. If we as imperfect parents look upon our imperfect children with pride and joy, just before awakening them, imagine how God must look upon us in Christ.

Physically, we don't have a breastpiece of precious stones to remind us of this reality as we pray, but we are to ask God to illumine the eyes of our inner spirit being to see this reality in the spiritual realm (Ephesians 1:18). It is through your intercession, as you begin to see those you are praying for as God sees them, that he will use you to raise up others as part of the kingdom of priests. The kingdom of God will become gloriously active on earth as the kingdom of priests becomes active in intercession. God can and will rule only through your intercession. It was for that reason that Christ died.

> *"You are worthy to take the scroll and break its seals and open it. For you were slaughtered, and your blood has ransomed people for God from every tribe and language and people and nation. And you have caused them to become a Kingdom of priests for our God. And they will reign on the earth" (NLT, Revelation 5:9, 10).*

If we do not see the kingdom of God vibrantly active in the communities, cities, and nations in which we live, it is because the church has not yet realized this vital truth. Only as the people of God organize and unite in intercession will we see his kingdom come, his will be done on earth as in heaven (Matthew 6:10). By this first call to morning prayer, we are to be conduits to synchronize what is happening on earth with what is happening in heaven. To do this, we must first believe that we will meet with the sovereign God as a result of the Lamb's sacrifice, and that we will hear from him. We must believe that God will honor, with his heavenly resources, every initiative we make in prayer. We must believe that he will illumine our eyes to see our church family as he sees them, without the filters of human prejudice, pride and competition. We will see and pray for them as they truly are in Christ: forgiven, loved, and transformed to be a kingdom of priests to rule on earth by prayer and intercession. One by one, those you have prayed for will join you in taking up their royal position seated with Christ in the heavenly realms as a mighty movement of prayer gets underway (Ephesians 2:6). It begins as you and I take our place of divine authority with Christ in intercession. It is a place in the heavenly realms which he reserved with his own blood.

Questions for Reflection:

1. Why do you think God established the early morning or 6 a.m. (and late afternoon or 6 p.m.) as the time when he would meet with his people and speak with them? (Exodus 29: 42, 43)

2. How will the understanding of your prayers as spiritual incense and an act of worship influence the way you pray? (Revelation 5: 8)

3. Explain how the symbol of the priest´s breastpiece will change the way you pray for other believers?

4. How does your identity as a member of Christ´s kingdom of priests motivate you to intercede for the world you live in? (Revelation 5: 9, 10)

The Third Hour (9 a.m.)

The next call to prayer is "The Third Hour" (9 a.m.). It was during this time that the believers were in the upper room praying, awaiting the promised kingdom anointing of the Holy Spirit to be witnesses of Christ's kingdom to the world (Acts 1:13: 2:1-4; 2:13-15). *"These men are not drunk, as you suppose. It's only nine in the morning" (Acts 2:15).* In the original language, what has been translated as "nine in the morning" reads "the third hour."[36] The Lord Jesus Christ, seated at the right hand of God, poured this anointing of the Spirit on them as evidence of his sovereignty and authority. *"Exalted to the right hand of God, he has received from the Father the promised Holy Spirit and has poured out what you now see and hear" (Acts 2:33).* They received this royal kingdom anointing so that they could begin to exercise their role as a kingdom of priests, not only interceding but also testifying to the reality of his kingdom. Their prayers and words would be confirmed by signs and wonders as evidence that King Jesus was indeed alive and at the right hand of God. (Mark 16:19, 20). The prayer of faith to receive the kingdom anointing of the Holy Spirit is as vitally important today as it was then. Jesus tells us how. *"If you then, though you*

At the third hour, Jesus was crucified. Fifty-two days later, at the third hour, he poured out the Holy Spirit.

---

36 Alfred Marshall, *The NRSV-NIV Parallel New Testament In Greek and English* (Grand Rapids, Michigan: Zondervan, 1990), p. 342.

are evil, know how to give good gifts to your children, how much more will your Father in heaven give the Holy Spirit to those who ask him" (Luke 11:13). The anointing is received by faith, as are all of God's gifts. However, true faith is manifested in persistent, persevering prayer as we have already learned. How many Christians today live without this kingdom anointing because they simply are not willing to exercise their faith as Jesus has commanded? God is faithful to his promises. The evidence is clear when we remember how the early disciples prayed and received the anointing of the Holy Spirit on the day of Pentecost. But, as leaky vessels we need to be filled again and again. The early believers did not only pray once for the kingdom anointing.

> *"Now, Lord, consider their threats and enable your servants to speak your word with great boldness. Stretch out your hand to heal and perform miraculous signs and wonders through the name of your holy servant Jesus." After they prayed, the place where they were meeting was shaken. And they were all filled with the Holy Spirit and spoke the word of God boldly (Acts 4:29-31).*

In addition to the kingdom anointing, as a kingdom of priests we also need the priestly anointing. Not only did Jesus pour out the royal kingdom anointing on his disciples at the third hour but he was also crucified for our sin at the third hour. *"It was the third hour when they crucified him" (Mark 15:25).* The danger of the kingdom anointing alone, with the signs of healing and other manifestations of the Spirit, is that we can forget its purpose. And power without purpose is dangerous. That is why we need the teaching from John's gospel to remind us of the priestly anointing that preceded the kingdom anointing of power. It happened on the day of the resurrection, fifty days before Pentecost.

> *"...Peace be with you!" After he said this, he showed them his hands and side. The disciples were overjoyed when they saw the Lord. Again Jesus said; "Peace be with you! As the Father has sent me, I am sending you." And with that he breathed on them and said, "Receive the Holy Spirit. If you forgive anyone his sins, they are forgiven; if you do not forgive them, they are not forgiven" (John 20:19b-23).*

Before Jesus gave them power, he gave them the anointing of forgiveness and commissioned them to take the message and lifestyle of forgiveness to others, just as he had brought it to them.

I believe that much of the modern North American church is living without the anointing of power and authority, the kingdom anointing, for one very important reason. We have forgotten that we have also been commissioned with the anointing of repentance and forgiveness, the priestly anointing. Jesus wants to ensure that we understand our commission in the Holy Spirit before we receive the power of the Holy Spirit. Jesus made this clear to his disciples prior to telling them to wait for the kingdom anointing of power:

> *"The Christ will suffer and rise from the dead on the third day, and repentance and forgiveness of sins will be preached in his name to all nations, beginning in Jerusalem. You are witnesses of these things. I am going to send you what my Father has promised; but stay in the city until you have been clothed with power from on high" (Luke 24:46-49).*

At the third hour, Jesus was crucified. Fifty-two days later, at the third hour, he poured out the Holy Spirit anointing of power. As we begin to exercise our new identity as a kingdom of priests in the early morning prayer, we would do well to remember to pray at 9 a.m. for a fresh anointing of the Spirit for ourselves and for the church. But let us remember the order of the anointing – the priestly anointing of forgiveness and then the kingdom anointing of power. Lack of repentance and forgiveness will block any outpouring of anointing power for healing or other manifestations of Christ's power.

The very name of our Lord in which we pray, "Jesus Christ", confirms this truth. The first name, Jesus, means *"...he will save his people from their sins" (Matthew 1:21)*. Christ means "anointed one, King" (Matthew 2:2, Luke 2:11). For our prayers to be heard and answered in the name of Jesus Christ, they must follow the divine titles for which the Son of God was sent. Jesus comes as the Priest of forgiveness and then as the King of power. James declares this in his letter as he writes about prayer: *"Therefore confess your sins to each other and pray for each other so that you may be healed. The prayer of a righteous man is powerful and effective" (James 5:16)*. The intercessor must be cleansed before he can be infused with power. The power of the resurrection confirms the truth of the cross.

The fulfillment of the rebuilding of the tabernacle of David is only realized in Christ as High Priest and King.[37] And it is realized in the Body of Christ as we remember and seek this double anointing. At the tabernacle of David, both king and priest were before the ark of God's presence ministering in prayer and praise. David appeared before the ark as king. However, it is interesting to note that, only on this occasion, he appeared not dressed in his royal robes but rather in the robes of the Levites. He was dressed as a priest wearing

---

37 Kevin J. Conner and Ken Malmin, *The Covenants: The Key To God's Relationship With Mankind* (Portland, Oregon: City Bible Publishing, 1983), p. 67.

the ephod. *"Now David was clothed in a robe of fine linen, as were all the Levites who were carrying the ark…David also wore a linen ephod" (1 Chronicles 15:27)*. It was a prophetic act concerning a future event. In Christ, the Son of David, the two offices were joined and are released through those he has redeemed to be a kingdom of priests. Christ's rule will be extended throughout the earth, not by military force, but through a powerful anointing of repentance and forgiveness. Then our message will be confirmed by a kingdom anointing of signs and wonders.

In studying the history of revivals, it should not surprise us that the primary characteristic of the move of the Holy Spirit has been that of deep repentance and forgiveness. Three of the four great principles of Robert Evans that sustained the Welsh revival and affected much of the world were focused on repentance:

1. All sin must be confessed to God and repented of. If there is anything in our lives about which there is even doubt as to whether it is good or evil – then cast it off!
2. There must be no cloud between the believer and God. Have you forgiven everybody? If not then don't expect forgiveness of your own sins.
3. We must obey the Holy Spirit. Do what the Holy Spirit prompts you to do. Prompt, implicit, unquestioning obedience…[38]

The preparation for Christ's first coming through the ministry of John the Baptist was evidenced by a mighty move of the Holy Spirit in repentance and forgiveness. The preparation for Christ's second coming

38 Rick Joyner, *The World Aflame* (Charlotte, NC: Morningstar Publications, 1993), pp. 39, 40.

will be no different. Christ first calls the churches of the last days to repentance in the book of Revelation (Revelation 2 and 3). He calls us to repent of our confidence in material things, of sexual immorality, and of losing our passion for him. He also calls us to persevere while suffering persecution, because there is a great reward for the overcomers. Amidst the growing darkness that is covering the nations, the light of his glorious presence will arise over these faithful ones (Isaiah 60:1-3). God will grant them power to push back the darkness in the nations (1 John 2:8). There will be a mighty move of repentance and revival that will sweep the globe. It is not far away. It is awaiting the united focused prayers and obedience of God's kingdom of priests.

Questions for Reflection:

1. Have you personally prayed for the anointing of the Holy Spirit? If so, what type of anointing did you anticipate?

2. How has the reality of the priestly anointing, as well as the royal kingdom anointing, influenced your faith with regard to the work of the Holy Spirit in your life?

3. How might this teaching bring healing and revival to your local church?

4. In what way might this teaching help to unite believers from other Christian backgrounds in prayer?

The Sixth Hour (12 noon)

The call to prayer at noon, the sixth hour, is equally significant. It was at this time, the lunch hour, that Peter prayed on the roof of the house of Simon the Tanner.

> *About noon the following day as they were on their journey and approaching the city, Peter went up on the roof to pray. He became hungry and wanted something to eat, and while the meal was being prepared, he fell into a trance (Acts 10:9).*

In the original text, the phrase that has been translated "noon" is actually "the sixth hour."[39] It was during this time that God revealed to Peter an amazing vision that would break all the paradigms that the early Jewish believers had about salvation in Christ and the covenant promises. They believed that, through their religious inheritance, the good news of Jesus Christ was exclusive property of the Jewish people (Ephesians 2:12). They rigidly carried out a list of religious and social practices that existed to ensure that Jew and Gentile did not mix. These served as a wall of separation, just like the wall in the temple that declared: "No foreigner may enter within the bar-

Is it any wonder that God called Peter to prayer at noon, commanding him to eat a meal that would open the doors for the good news of Jesus Christ to all nations and peoples?

39 Marshall, p. 372.

ricade which surrounds the temple and enclosure. Anyone who is caught doing so will have himself to thank for his ensuing death."[40] The warning of that sign was intended for all Gentiles - including you and me.

The vision that God gave Peter broke all the previous presuppositions. God commanded him to eat food that, until that time, had been Gentile food, which was unclean for Jews. God's words to Peter were: *"Do not call anything impure that God has made clean." (Acts 10:15)*. The message was clear: the good news of salvation and of the covenant promises was for the Gentiles as well. In Jesus Christ, they were no longer unclean before God. At that very moment, some servants of a Roman centurion arrived to take Peter to the centurion's house to share the news of salvation in Christ.

This paradigm-breaking event at noon was not the first. Many years earlier, Jesus himself sat down at a well in Samaria at noon.

> *Now he had to go through Samaria. So he came to a town in Samaria called Sychar, near the plot of ground Jacob had given to his son Joseph. Jacob's well was there, and Jesus, tired as he was from the journey, sat down by the well. It was about <u>the sixth hour</u> (John 4:4-6).*

The statement – "Jesus had to go through Samaria"- was not a geographical necessity, but rather a spiritual one. All Jews avoided Samaria, the "unclean province", by travelling around it to get to Galilee. Even though half-Jew, the Samaritans were considered to be as unclean as the Gentiles. They were no longer considered Jewish, but Gentile, because of their mixed blood and mixed beliefs. Jesus' determination to go through Sa-

---

40 F.F. Bruce, *The New Testament Documents: Are They Reliable?* (Downers Grove, Ilinois: Intervarsity Press, 1981), p. 95.

maria would have shocked the disciples. Jesus was not satisfied with merely breaking through geographical boundaries; his aim was to break down social, and more importantly, spiritual boundaries. So it was, at the sixth hour, that Jesus sat down at a well to talk with an "impure" Samaritan. To add insult to injury, he chose a woman; even worse, a morally loose woman. This would have been unheard of for any Jewish man at that time, and much less for a rabbi. After identifying her need of repentance, Jesus offered her the gift of salvation and of the Holy Spirit.

In this event, we dare not lose sight of the context. It was at the sixth hour, lunch time, when all of the disciples had one thing in mind…food! Doesn't that also happen with us, as our physical appetites take priority over the spiritual? The disciples were hungry. Jesus was just as physically hungry, tired and weak as they were (John 4:6,8). However, his interest was not in lunch. When the disciples returned, they were wide-eyed with disbelief as they discovered him sharing the good news of the kingdom with a Samaritan woman. They said to him: *"Rabbi, eat something" (John 4:31).* But Jesus' response pointed to a heavenly appetite and a heavenly lunch that he was thoroughly enjoying.

> *"I have food to eat that you know nothing about"..."My food", said Jesus, "is to do the will of him who sent me and to finish his work. Do you not say, 'Four months more and then the harvest'? I tell you, open your eyes and look at the fields! They are ripe for harvest" (John 4:32-35).*

The timing of this event and that of Peter's prayer on the roof is no mere coincidence. There is a critical spiritual lesson for our own prayer and resulting obedience as we think of the noon hour. When our physical appetites begin to call, heaven is also calling.

For it was beginning at this sixth hour, as Jesus was hardly able to move, nailed to the cross, that a thick darkness came over the land.

> *From the sixth hour until the ninth hour darkness came over all the land. About the ninth hour Jesus cried out in a loud voice: "Eloi, Eloi, lama sabachthani?" – which means, "My God, my God, why have you forsaken me?" (Matthew 27:45-46).*

It was beginning at the sixth hour, as a supernatural darkness covered the land, that Jesus the Lamb of God took on himself the sin of the world (John 1:29). God laid upon him the iniquity of us all (Isaiah 53:6), Jew and Gentile alike.

Is it any wonder that Jesus chose the noon hour to challenge the disciples' priorities and prejudices, summoning them to a harvest among the very ones they had socially excluded? Is it any wonder that God called Peter to prayer at noon, commanding him to eat a meal that would open the doors for the good news of Jesus Christ to all nations and peoples? Is it any wonder that we should consider praying at noon to bring our appetite in line with that of Jesus Christ and the early believers?

May our appetite become like that of Peter, and of Jesus - interceding at noon for the nations, breaking through boundaries that have hindered the good news of Christ. And we must be ready to put feet to our prayers.

> *Then he said to his disciples, "The harvest is plentiful but the workers are few. Ask the Lord of the harvest, therefore, to send out workers into his harvest field." (Matthew 9:37,38).*

Jesus asked his disciples to pray that the Lord of the harvest would send out workers; then, Jesus sent the very ones he had asked to pray. One of the greatest benefits of praying for the harvest of the nations is that Jesus will also give us the authority to do the very work we have prayed for.

Do you remember that separating wall at the temple with its sign of doom for the Gentiles? It declared an impassable separation between us and God! One day at the temple, just outside of the separating wall, some Greek Gentiles approached the disciples of Jesus and asked if they could see him. *" 'Sir,' they said, 'we would like to see Jesus' " (John 12:21).* Listen to Jesus' response: *"The hour has come for the Son of Man to be glorified....Now my heart is troubled, and what shall I say? 'Father, save me from this hour'? No, it was for this very reason I came to this hour" (John 12:23,27).* It was the desire of the Gentiles to see Jesus that signalled the hour for the Lamb of God to take on himself the sin of the world. It was the hour that would forever bring down the separating wall and open the way to God for the nations (Ephesians 2:14-16). Next time you have lunch, remember that it was this hour that changed your destiny. Will you be part of a prayer movement to intercede at noon for the destiny of the nations?

Questions for Reflection:

1. We often associate food with a certain culture or nationality. How did God use the noon-hour meal to reveal his will for the nations to Peter? (Acts 10:9-16)

2. Why do you think Jesus chose the noon-hour meal to reveal to his disciples his passion to reach out to the non-Jews? (John 4: 32-35)

3. How will Jesus' passion to reach you change the way you think about your passions and priorities?

4. God was creative in how he communicated the noon message concerning the nations. What might be some creative ways for making 12 noon a significant time for you and your church to pray for the nations?

The Ninth Hour (3 p.m.)

The call to pray at the ninth hour, three in the afternoon, was an established temple prayer hour for the Jewish people. When Peter and John healed a paralytic at "the Beautiful Gate", in the name of Jesus (Acts 3:2), they did it while on the way to afternoon prayer. *"One day Peter and John were going up to the temple at the time of prayer – at three in the afternoon" (Acts 3:1).* In the original language the phrase "three in the afternoon" reads "the ninth hour."[41]

It was at the ninth hour, or 3 p.m., that the veil which covered the Holy of Holies was torn in two by the hand of God himself.

There is Old Testament evidence for the daytime prayers at sunrise and sunset (the hours of incense). There is also evidence of noon prayer in David's discipline of praying at sunrise, noon, and sunset. However, there is no clear Old Testament evidence of when and how the tradition of afternoon prayer became established. We do know that Daniel prayed three times a day, praying at another established time other than the two hours of incense (Daniel 6:10-12). It is possible from this inference that the afternoon prayer hour already existed prior to the early church. It is also possible that, like David, he prayed at noon. Whatever the case, it is clear that by the time of Christ and the early believers, afternoon prayer at the ninth hour was officially recognized in the call to prayer.

---

41 Marshall, p. 345.

In addition to Peter and John's example, we discover Cornelius, the Roman centurion who loved God, praying faithfully at three in the afternoon.

> *At Caesarea there was a man named Cornelius, a centurion in what was known as the Italian Regiment. He and all his family were devout and God-fearing; he gave generously to those in need and prayed to God regularly. One day at about three in the afternoon he had a vision. He distinctly saw an angel of God, who came to him and said: "Cornelius!"(Acts 10:1-3).*

It was at this specific time that Cornelius was told by the angel to send men to Joppa to the home where Peter was staying. Peter would return and explain to Cornelius the good news of salvation in Christ. The way had been opened for Cornelius and for all Gentiles to receive forgiveness and to be reconciled with God through Jesus Christ. Why did God send an angel to answer Cornelius' prayer at the ninth hour? Why is the author specific about this time? The reason is profoundly simple and yet life-transforming. The work of Christ on the cross weaves its way through all of the hours of the prayer clock. That cannot be overemphasized, especially in the ninth-hour call to prayer.

Matthew, Jesus' disciple, describes the divine significance of this hour. This revelation should move us to be as excited as the angel who was sent to speak to Cornelius during afternoon prayer (3 p.m.).

> *About the ninth hour Jesus cried out in a loud voice, "Eloi, Eloi, lama sabachthani?" – which means "My God, my God, why have you forsaken me?"...And when Jesus had cried out again in a loud voice, he gave up his spirit. At that moment the curtain of the temple was torn in two from top to bottom (Matthew 27:46, 50, 51).*

It was at the ninth hour that the veil which covered the Holy of Holies was torn in two by the hand of God himself. By this act God was declaring that, once and for all, through Christ's sacrifice, the price had been paid for sin. Forgiveness and reconciliation were now extended by God to all. Direct access to the throne of God's grace was open for everyone. The reality of a new way into the presence of God in Christ is stated clearly in the book of Hebrews.

> *Therefore, brothers, since we have confidence to enter the Most Holy Place by the blood of Jesus, by a new and living way opened for us through the curtain, that is, his body, and since we have a great priest over the house of God, let us draw near to God with a sincere heart in full assurance of faith (Hebrews 10:19-21).*

> *Let us then approach the throne of grace with confidence, so that we may receive mercy and find grace to help us in our time of need (Hebrews 4:16).*

Above all the calls to prayer, the ninth hour (3 p.m.) invites us to experience the new privilege of our direct access to God's presence. Twice, Moses climbed a mountain and fasted forty days, crying out to God to show him his glory. He pleaded with God that his presence go with them as a nation. God listened and his presence accompanied them, but always with the reminder that they could not come into his presence because of sin. The veil was in place and the way was not yet open. Once a year, the high priest would appear before the ark of God's presence with the blood of a spotless sacrifice. It was a prophetic ceremony looking forward to the day when Jesus would appear with his own sacrificed blood before God, and forever remove the separation of guilt and shame. He would open the new way of direct access to God.

We do not need to climb Mount Sinai or fast forty days to come into God's glorious presence. We can enter humbly, with full confidence that we will be received by him. The tabernacle of David without its veil was a prophetic symbol of the divine favor that is now granted to us. So David could write with certainty: *"The sacrifices of God are a broken spirit; a broken spirit and contrite heart, O God, you will not despise" (Psalm 51:17).* The 3 p.m. call to prayer should be a daily spiritual exercise when we thankfully walk into God's presence through the new and living way offered in Christ. It is the only way that is open to God, as we come through faith in Christ's provision and leave no unconfessed sin in the way. It is a time when we can enjoy God's presence and our new relationship with him as his children and his chosen ones.

While we are enjoying our reconciled relationship with him, we must remember where we are and who we are with. We are before the throne of God and in the presence of King Jesus. God's love for us in Christ and our love for him has kingdom implications. True kingdom love is reflected in worship and service. God commanded Pharaoh through Moses: *"Let my people go, so that they may worship me" (Exodus 9:1)*. In one version, it is translated "worship" (NIV) while in another it is translated "serve" (KJV). The reason is that the Hebrew word "abad" for "worship" also means "serve".[42] In the New Testament, the Greek word often used for "worship" is "latreia" which also means "service."[43] The implications are obvious. Just as God rescued and freed the Israelites from Egypt to worship and serve him, so too we have been rescued from the dominion of darkness for that

---

42 J. Strong, "abad," (Strong's Hebrew # 05647).

43 J. Strong, "latreia," (Strong's Greek # 2999).

same purpose. The Apostle Paul emphasizes this truth.

> *And God raised us up with Christ and seated us with him in the heavenly realms in Christ Jesus...For it is by grace you have been saved, through faith –and this is not from yourselves, it is the gift of God- not by works, so that no one can boast. For we are God's workmanship, created in Christ Jesus to do good works, which God prepared in advance for us to do (Ephesians 2:6, 8-10).*

We come before the throne to worship him and we leave his throne to serve him in the works he has prepared for us from before time. The purpose for which we have been made and saved is to worship and serve him.

The fact that God has given us access to his throne and his kingdom makes us kingdom representatives. We are to be agents to extend his kingdom to the world in which we live. The children of Israel had created in their minds a dichotomy between their worship of God and their daily activity in the society in which they lived. They committed a fateful mistake that the modern church has also committed. The voice of God through the prophet Isaiah emphasizes this.

> *"When you spread out your hands in prayer, I will hide my eyes from you; even if you offer many prayers, I will not listen....Stop doing wrong, learn to do right! Seek justice, encourage the oppressed. Defend the cause of the fatherless, plead the case of the widow. 'Come now let us reason together,' says the Lord. 'Though your sins are like scarlet, they shall be as white as snow; though they are red as crimson, they shall be like wool' "(Isaiah 1:15,16-18).*

The concept of the throne and the kingdom of God will

not permit such a dichotomy.

Today, the younger generations feel this conviction and are taking steps to correct the dichotomy. They have perceived the error of a personalized gospel that is primarily centered on the well-being of the individual without any accountability to the needs of the community and the world in which we live. The Church of the last generations before Christ's return will truly worship God in a lifestyle of prayer and repentance. That repentance will be reflected in service that not only speaks boldly about Christ's kingdom but also does acts of justice that reflect his kingdom. When we lift our hands in prayer before the throne of grace and righteousness, we must remember God's words to us through the prophet Isaiah and through the Apostle Paul. Prayer without obedient action will not reach the heavenly realms. As we come near to God, we must not forget that we have been saved for a great and glorious purpose - to worship and to serve him by doing the works of righteousness and justice that he has prepared for us from eternity past.

Questions for Reflection:

1. Three p.m. was an established prayer time in Jewish religious practice. How did that time take on a significance of immeasurable proportion for the prayers of the early church? (Matthew 27: 46, 50, 51)

2. What evidence is there of the spiritual impact of Christ´s work at 3 p.m. and the results of praying at 3 p.m.? (Acts 3:1-10; Acts 10:1-8)

3. Reflect on the Father tearing the veil and Christ opening a new and living way to his Father´s presence. How will these images impact the way you pray at 3 p.m.? (Hebrews 10:19-21, 4:16)

4. How can we be sure that our prayers in Christ's name truly reflect and manifest God's throne and his kingdom to the world in which we live?

The First Watch (6 p.m.)

Just as sunrise was the signal for the call to prayer at the morning "hour of incense", so sunset was the call to prayer at the evening hour of incense. It was the hour when the priest entered the Holy Place to light the lamp that was before the Lord (Exodus 30:8). He was to offer incense and intercede for the people. As previously mentioned, with the Roman 24-hour clock and the 3-hour blocks of time, the evening hour of incense became the call to prayer at 6 p.m. It was the beginning of the first of four night watches. The Jewish people took seriously the need to watch in prayer, because God had watched over them the night that they were led out of Egypt (Exodus 12:42). *"He will not let your foot slip – he who watches over you will not slumber; indeed, he who watches over Israel will neither slumber nor sleep" (Psalm 121:3,4).* When we take seriously the concept of night vigils of prayer, watching in the spiritual realm for ourselves and on behalf of others, we are joining our hearts with God's vigilant heart.

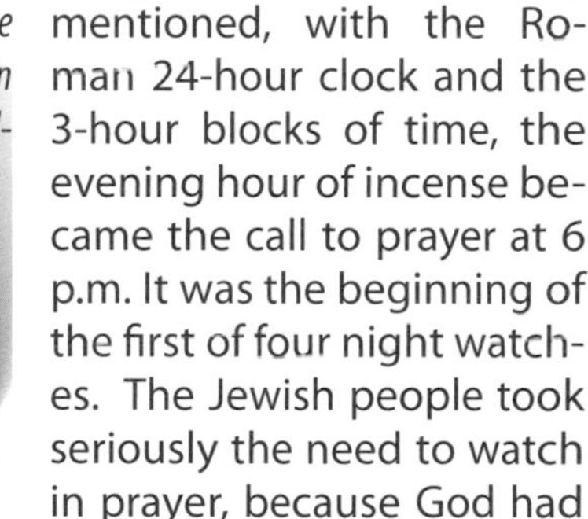

When Jesus prayed for his disciples and for us, as his new children, he was fulfilling the instruction in Lamentations to pray for the children in the first watch of the night.

Jesus emphasized the critical importance of the prayer watches in the life of his followers.

> *"Therefore keep watch because you do not know when the owner of the house will come back – whether in the*

> *evening, or at midnight, or when the rooster crows, or at dawn. If he comes suddenly, do not let him find you sleeping. What I say to you, I say to everyone: 'Watch!'" (Mark 13:35-37).*

Note that Jesus mentions four prayer watches during the night that have to do with the Roman night watches. The first 3-hour watch ended at dusk (evening, or 9 p.m.). The second ended at midnight. The third ended at the time the Romans called the "cock crows" or 3 a.m. It was not actually a cock crowing. The Roman soldier assigned to that watch sounded a trumpet two times to signal the end of the second last watch and to signal the beginning of the last watch.[44] For that reason, the third watch was called "the rooster crows". The important thing to note is that Jesus emphasized all of the watches in terms of prayer, beginning with the first watch.

The first watch that began at 6 p.m. and terminated at approximately dusk, or "evening" as the NIV reads, would have been the time that Jesus celebrated the Passover meal or the last supper. While the Roman day began and ended at sunrise, the Jewish day began and ended at sundown (6 p.m.). The Passover Sabbath would have begun at 6 p.m. on Friday evening.[45] The Passover meal was celebrated during this first watch. It was celebrated as a family, the parents with the children, as a way of fulfilling God's command that the deliverance of Passover be remembered from one generation to another (Exodus 12:26,27)[46]. The story would

---

44 Alister McGrath, "New Testament," *Christianity: An Introduction* (Malden, Mass.: Blackwell Publishing, 2006), p. 89.

45 Jesus would have celebrated the Passover meal with his disciples on Thursday, rather than the normal Friday evening so that he could offer himself as the true Passover Lamb on the Friday.

46 Eric Peter Lipson, *Passover Haggadah* (San Francisco: JFJ Publishing, 1986), p. 8.

have been told of how God watched over the Israelites, protecting them from the Angel of Death through the blood of the lamb that they had painted on their doorposts. Then he watched over them and protected them from Pharaoh as they were freed and led out of Egypt.

That night with Jesus, however, the meaning of the Passover meal was to be revealed in its fullest sense as the true Passover Lamb celebrated with God's true children (John 13:33). The Passover Lamb was no longer a symbol of remembrance but a living reality. The supper ended with Jesus praying for his disciples and for us, that God would watch over us and protect us from Satan and sin in this new deliverance (John 17:15). Above all, he prayed that we would remain united in love (John 17: 23, 24). When Jesus prayed for his disciples and for us, as the new children, he was also fulfilling the instruction in Lamentations to pray for the children in the first watch of the night.

> *Arise, cry out in the night, as the watches of the night begin; pour out your heart like water in the presence of the Lord. Lift up your hands to him for the lives of your children, who faint from hunger at the head of every street (Lamentations 2:19).*

Not only did Jesus pray in fulfillment of this passage, but he offered himself as the bread of the new covenant for the children – the only bread that could satisfy our hunger. He is the children's bread that brings life and healing (Mark 7:27; John 6:48-50).

In focusing on the first watch, it is important to note that Zechariah's ministry of intercession in the Holy Place (Luke 1:8-10) could have been either in the morning or in the evening hour of incense. However, the fact that the archangel Gabriel came with a message to Zechariah in response to his prayers for a child indicates that it was most likely the evening hour of incense (the first watch), when prayers and intercession were offered specifically for the children.

> *"Do not be afraid Zechariah; your prayer has been heard. Your wife Elizabeth will bear you a son, and you are to give him the name John. He will be a joy and delight to you, and many will rejoice because of his birth, for he will be great in the sight of the Lord. He is never to take wine or other fermented drink, and he will be filled with the Holy Spirit even from birth. Many of the people of Israel will he bring back to the Lord their God. And he will go before the Lord, in the spirit and power of Elijah, to turn the hearts of the fathers to their children and the disobedient to the wisdom of the righteous – to make ready a people prepared for the Lord" (Luke 1: 13 – 17).*

Gabriel came with a response that was far beyond what Zechariah could ever have dreamed. They had assumed that God had forgotten them. Yet, not only would they have a child, their child would be the forerunner to the Savior. He would go before the Messiah to prepare the way for salvation.

This should motivate us as we pray for the next generations, knowing that God desires to respond to us so that our prayers are merged with his great plans. God's plan for our children, whether physical or spiritual, is not just that they be ordinary children but that their lives be powerful in extending his kingdom and in preparing the world for the Second Coming of Christ. God is looking for more forerunners like John. Jesus said this:

> *"I tell you the truth: Among those born of women there has not risen anyone greater than John the Baptist; yet he who is least in the kingdom of heaven is greater than he. From the days of John the Baptist until now,*

the kingdom of heaven has been forcefully advancing and forceful men lay hold of it" (Matthew 11:11,12).

Zechariah prayed with little faith, but he prayed. And God responded beyond all expectations.

As we seek to respond to the "Zechariah call" of praying for the children, and releasing God´s plan and potential in their lives, we need to carefully reflect on our part in that plan as parents (physical or spiritual). Note the words of the angel in response to Zechariah´s prayers: *"And he will go in the spirit of Elijah, to turn the hearts of the fathers to their children and the disobedient to the wisdom of the righteous – to make ready a people for the Lord" (Luke 1:17).* In this declaration, the archangel Gabriel was quoting and declaring the fulfillment of the very last prophecy of the Old Testament in Malachi 4:6. It was to be fulfilled through Zechariah's son, John. The only variation from the prophecy in Malachi is that Gabriel replaced the words *"the hearts of the children to their fathers"* with *"the disobedient to the wisdom of the righteous".* The archangel Gabriel revealed that disobedience, rebellion and sin in one generation have their roots in the broken relationships with the previous generation. God's plan was that John would be an instrument for bringing repentance and righteousness. He was to reconcile relationships between the fathers and their children. It was this ministry that would prepare the way for Christ's first coming. Zechariah knew that he had a part to play if the prophesied ministry was to be fulfilled in his son.

The best way to initiate reconciliation with our children is to pray for them, so that God will move in our hearts and in theirs, turning our hearts toward each other. When we are reconciled with our children, the way will be open for God to use them to bring repentance and revival to their generation. God used Zechariah's prayers to release a powerful ministry of repentance and reconciliation through his son. We have the same opportunity with our children.

May the first watch be a time when we pray for protection and deliverance from Satan and sin for the next generations. We need to pray that they will be powerfully anointed as forerunners in preparing the world for Christ's Second Coming. But that can only happen in prayer as our hearts turn toward them and their hearts to us in reconciliation and repentance. Pray for reconciliation of the generations and for unity among them. Then the next generations will forcefully lay hold of the kingdom, synchronizing heaven and earth and activating God's will in human affairs on earth. May his will be done on earth as it is in heaven through the next generations of believers! But remember your part!

Questions for Reflection:

1. Have you ever been part of a church that has practised "watching prayer" or prayer vigils? Explain some of your prayer watch experiences.

2. The lessons of Passover and of the first watch were specifically directed at the children and included them in the context of a meal (Exodus 12: 26, 27; Lamentations 2:19). How could "first watch" prayer for the children be structured in a creative way around the evening meal to invite their participation?

3. Not only is prayer to be directed at our physical children, but also at our spiritual children. Who are the spiritual children that God has put into your care?

4. What is the spiritual potential that you are beginning to see with your eyes of faith for each one of your physical and spiritual children (2 Corinthians 5:16, 17)?

5. Why do you think reconciliation needs to be a key theme as we pray for our children (physical or spiritual)?

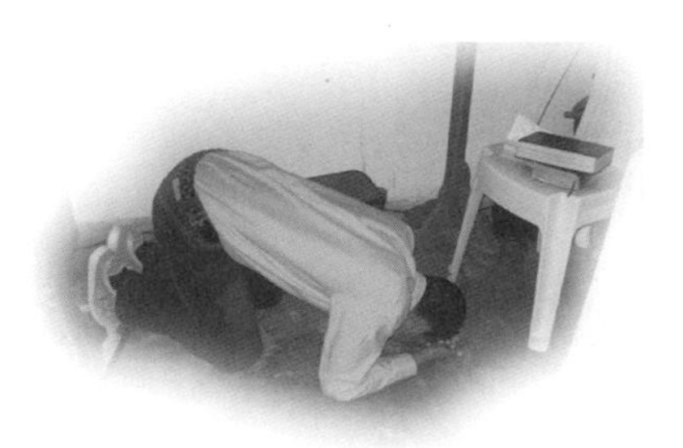

The Second Watch (9 p.m.)

At nine p.m. or dusk, the second watch began, lasting until midnight. This appears to be the watch of spiritual preparation, when Jesus had the custom of going to the Mount of Olives to pray in the weeks leading up to his death. It was a custom that he carried on right up to the night before his crucifixion. *"Jesus went out as usual to the Mount of Olives, and his disciples followed him" (Luke 22:39).* During this watch, from dusk until midnight, Jesus taught his disciples the importance of prayer in order to escape the corruption of the world and to be faithful to him until the end.

It was in prayer on the Mount of Olives, during the second watch, that Jesus overcame Satan and subjected his own will to that of his Father.

> *"Be always on the watch, and pray that you may be able to escape all that is about to happen, and that you may be able to stand before the Son of Man." Each day Jesus was teaching at the temple, and each evening he went out to spend the night on the hill called the Mount of Olives (Luke 21:36,37).*

This was the watch when Jesus exhorted Peter and the other disciples to pray, knowing that their faith would be severely tested a few hours later.

> *Then he returned to his disciples and found them sleeping. "Could you men not keep watch* <u>*with me*</u> *for one hour?" he asked Peter. "Watch and pray so that you will not fall into temptation. The spirit is willing, but the body is weak." (Matthew 26:40, 41).*

The second watch is the prayer watch of spiritual preparation with Christ himself. We are never to pray alone. We must come to him and join with him in our prayers. If we are going to be more than conquerors in Christ over the temptations and tests of the flesh and the enemy, we have to subject the flesh to his will through watching prayer. Having asked the disciples to pray with him, Jesus came back after the first hour to check up on them, and found them asleep. He was upset that they could not even pray the first hour of the watch with him. He went to pray again and, when he returned, he discovered that they were still sleeping. Without saying a word, he went back to pray the last hour of the watch (Matthew 26:43-44). By then, it was too late for Peter and the others. The enemy had arrived and the test was about to begin.

Jesus' prayer gives us clear teaching about praying the watches. He prayed during the three hours of the watch, but after each hour he checked in with the others to encourage them in their prayer. As we commit to pray with Christ, he will check in on us to encourage us. When he does, we need to respond and not ignore his call. To ignore his call is to run the risk of being unprepared for the test. There have been times when I have become drowsy in my prayer and I have heard a voice that has jolted me awake. As I look at this passage, I have no doubt that it was Jesus awakening me to pray at least one hour with him.

It was in prayer on the Mount of Olives, during the second watch, that Jesus overcame Satan and subjected his own will to the will of his Father (Matthew 26:39,42). *"Going a little farther, he fell with his face to the ground and prayed, 'My Father, if it is possible, may this cup be taken from me. Yet not as I will, but as you will' " (Matthew 26:39).* The temptation for Jesus was great. In his human nature, he felt the incredible pull to run from the cross and leave us with our sin. But, in prayer he won the pivotal battle of human history. He submitted his will to his Father and walked resolutely to the cross. It is only as we pray with Jesus that our will can be subjected to his. The author of Hebrews affirms that after Jesus had finished fulfilling his Father's will on the cross, he sat down at the right hand of his Father. He then says: *"Since that time he waits for his enemies to be made his footstool" (Hebrews 10:13).* To understand more clearly this verse, we also need to read 2 Corinthians 10:4, 5:

> *The weapons we fight with are not the weapons of the world. On the contrary, they have divine power to demolish strongholds. We demolish arguments and every pretension that sets itself up against the knowledge of God, and we take captive every thought to make it obedient to Christ.*

Christ is waiting for us to take action against specific enemies. Satan, the flesh, and the world will ultimately be brought to complete subjection as we, in Christ, tear down their power base of rebellious thought strongholds. The deadly enemies that would destroy us are not outside of us but are inside our mind and heart. These enemies are demonically-empowered fleshly desires and thoughts that war against the Spirit of God so that we will not carry out God's will. *"For the sinful nature desires what is contrary to the Spirit, and the Spirit what is contrary to the sinful nature. They are in conflict with each other, so that you do not do what you want" (Galatians 5:17).*

Jesus has given us the answer to victory over the flesh. It is not through becoming more active in ministry. It is not through attempting to be more disciplined and self-controlled. It is through joining him in prayer before the Father. *"Therefore he is able to save completely those who come to God through him, because he always lives to intercede for them" (Hebrews 7:25).* Jesus overcame Satan and sin in prayer. We can overcome Satan and sin by joining Christ in prayer, and merging our wills with his before the Father. *"Because he himself suffered when he was tempted, he is able to help those who are being tempted" (Hebrews 2:18).* Each time we choose to say "no" to the call to serve the flesh with its passion for food, entertainment, material possesions, etc. and choose to dedicate time to prayer with Christ, we weaken the flesh. Satan and the flesh know that it is prayer that connects us to the Holy Spirit and to the power of Christ.

What greater joy could there be than to respond to Christ's invitation to pray with him - the One who lives to intercede for us? Jesus is our great High Priest who has redeemed us to be a kingdom of priests through which he will rule the earth. Nothing excites him more than when we respond to his call to prayer, asking him to teach us as we pray alongside him. With him, in prayer, we receive all the divine resources we need for living a holy life and receiving a transformed character.

> *His divine power has given us everything we need for life and godliness through our knowledge of him who called us by his own glory and goodness. Through these he has given us his very great and precious promises, so that through them you may participate in the divine nature and escape the corruption in the world caused by evil desires (2 Peter 1:3,4).*

We need to shake off the spiritual cobwebs and respond to his call.

I remember keeping watch at night in my military days and having to be quite creative to keep myself and my companions awake and alert. We were very alert for the first half hour or so, expecting the attack at any moment. However, as time went on, even though the attack was still imminent, our state of alertness slowly weakened, and drowsiness set in. You may need to walk around, lift up your hands, pray out loud or read Scripture as you pray in order to get the blood circulating and the soul stirred. Sitting and passively praying in our minds is often the quickest way to become distracted and drowsy. The devil is well aware of our weaknesses, and his strategy is to wait for an opportune time to attack (Luke 4). We need to take the positions of prayer warriors, and like the soldier who is on watch, do everything possible to keep ourselves vigilant at Christ's side.

Questions for Reflection:

1. According to Jesus' teaching in Luke 21:36-37, explain the necessity of "watching prayer" and prayer vigils in the life of the church.

2. Why do you think Christ specifies the amount of time in his invitation for Peter to pray the watch with him? (Matthew 26: 40, 41)

3. Knowing that the spirit is willing but the body is weak, what is the victory that Christ will grant us by heeding his invitation to pray the night watch with him? (See Matthew 26:39; Philippians 2:13; Hebrews 2: 18)

4. Read and meditate on Hebrews 7:25. How does this verse encourage you to join Christ in prayer and intercession?

The Third Watch (12 Midnight)

While the second watch focuses on spiritual preparation for battle, the third watch (beginning at midnight) appears to be the watch of actual spiritual battle. It is when our preparation and spiritual foundations are put to the test in battle conditions. In the New Testament, this watch of spiritual battle lasted until 3 a.m., when the cock crowed. The cock was the Roman soldier who sounded the trumpet two times signalling the end of the second last watch. This was the watch when Satan's petition to sift Peter like wheat was fulfilled (Luke 22:31-34).

The second and third watches of spiritual preparation and battle are extremely important to the Lord Jesus. He mentions them specifically in the context of rewarding those who persevere in their spiritual responsibilities.

In the first watch during the Passover meal, when Jesus prayed for them as children that God would protect them from Satan (John 17), Peter boasted that he would follow Jesus to death. Jesus told Peter that, instead of following him to death, Peter would deny him. *"But he replied: 'Lord I am willing to go with you to prison and to death.' Jesus answered: 'I tell you, Peter, before the rooster crows today, you will deny three times that you know me' " (Luke 22:33,34).* Jesus was declaring that Peter did not yet have the spiritual preparedness to overcome the desires and will of the flesh that warred within him.

In the second watch, Jesus invited Peter and

the others to pray with him, warning them that even though their spirit was willing, only through prayer could the flesh be overcome. It would only happen by praying with Jesus, submitting their wills to the Father (Matthew 26:38-45). But Peter neglected the invitation and the outcome was tragic.

> *About an hour later another asserted, "Certainly this fellow was with him, for he is a Galilean." Peter replied, "Man, I don't know what you're talking about!" Just as he was speaking, the rooster crowed. The Lord turned and looked straight at Peter. Then Peter remembered the word the Lord had spoken to him: "Before the rooster crows today, you will disown me three times." And he went outside and wept bitterly (Luke 22:59-62).*

Each test and trial that comes our way has the potential to either become a character crisis or a character-building experience depending on our spiritual preparation. These tests are meant to be constructive instruments in God's hands to shape and mature our faith (Romans 5:1-5, 2 Corinthians 4:16-17, James 1:2-5). God has planned for us to be tested, just as Abraham was tested (Genesis 22), and Moses and the people of Israel were tested: *"In this way I will test them and see whether they will follow my instructions" (Exodus 16:4b).* Jesus promises that we will be tested. After giving us his kingdom commands in the Sermon on the Mount, Jesus concludes by saying that tests will certainly come. We will stand firm in the storms of life, like a house built on a solid foundation of rock, if we obey his commands. If not, like a house built on a precarious foundation of sand, we will fall (Matthew 7:24-27). Although we will surely be tested, we can see that Jesus is committed to equipping us and helping us to pass the test. For that to happen we need to be in prayer with him.

We can learn from Peter's error. If we are prepared through prayer with Christ, we can expect to win the battle against the enemy. This was the case with Paul and Silas when they were imprisoned, chained, whipped and beaten.

> *About midnight Paul and Silas were praying and singing hymns to God, and the other prisoners were listening to them. Suddenly there was such a violent earthquake that the foundations of the prison were shaken. At once all the prison doors flew open, and everybody's chains came loose (Acts 16:25,26).*

The second and third watches of spiritual preparation and spiritual battle are extremely important to the Lord Jesus. He mentions them specifically in the context of rewarding those who persevere in their spiritual responsibilities.

> *"It will be good for those servants whose master finds them watching when he comes. I tell you the truth, he will dress himself to serve, will have them recline at the table and will come and wait on them. It will be good for those servants whose master finds them ready, even if he comes in the second or third watch of the night" (Luke 12:37,38).*

The moment we are born into the kingdom, we are born into a spiritual battlefield. This was true with Jesus, whose life Satan sought to devour and destroy as soon as he was born (Revelation 12:4). The persecution of believers that is happening in many locations around the globe is evidence of an intense battle taking place. Shortly after being created, Adam and Eve found themselves in mortal combat with the serpent, the devil, in the Garden of Eden. They failed and the human race fell with them. But in the Garden of Gethsemane, on the Mount of Olives, Jesus secured the victory by praying and interceding during the last hours before he was arrested, tried and crucified on Mount Calvary. Having prepared himself spiritually, he was ready to stand firm, resolute to the finish. The tests and trials will come. The question is whether or not we will be ready to take a firm stand.

The Apostle Paul shares the secret of being able to stand firm in our spiritual battle: *"Finally, be strong in the Lord and in his mighty power. Put on the full armor of God so that you can take your stand against the devil's schemes" (Ephesians 6:10).* Peter's mistake was that he assumed he could stand firm in his own strength and determination. But, he soon discovered that these were useless in spiritual warfare. Earthly power is of no use for spiritual battles. Only heavenly power is effective in heavenly battles. *" 'Not by might, nor by power, but by my Spirit,' says the Lord Almighty" (Zechariah 4:6)*. Paul and the prophet Zechariah remind us that our strength for this battle must come from God and from his mighty power. We are to be "strong in the Lord" and not in ourselves. So Paul declares that God has actually prepared for each one of us his special armor, particularly designed to deal with all of the enemy's weapons, strategies and schemes against us. Now in Christ we have the battle advantage, but only in his power and with his armor. Jesus himself demonstrates the use of this armor in his preparation and test in the wilderness prior to beginning his ministry. Led by the Holy Spirit, he began a time of prayer and fasting in a solitary place. At the end of forty days, the devil arrived to test him. Satan discovered that, while Jesus had been weakened physically, he had been strengthened spiritually and wielded the sword of the Spirit, the Word of God, with incredible power and effectiveness in defeating him (Matthew 4).

As a church and as individuals, we must take seriously the call to pray during the second and third prayer watches. We must clothe ourselves with the armor of God to guarantee the victory in the battles with the enemy of our soul (Ephesians 6:10-20). The armor of God described by Paul is often neglected as an instrument of prayer. The Lord gives us this armor not only as spiritual protection but also as a powerful offensive weapon. The offensive weapons mentioned are his Word and his Spirit. They can only be unleashed against the enemy in prayer. *"Take the helmet of salvation and the sword of the Spirit, which is the Word of God. And pray in the Spirit on all occasions with all kinds of prayers and requests. With this in mind, be alert…" (Ephesians 6:17,18).* In the original language, the word "alert" means "keep watch" or "keep awake".[47] Paul and Silas entered the battle watch prepared and won the battle in Christ's name. Many Christians in North America are living defeated spiritual lives because they have ignored the armor that Christ has provided for them in the prayer closet.

We are meant to approach God's throne and kneel before the King with the Word before us, his kingdom constitution in our hearts. If we come before him without praying his Word, we are coming before him without the sword of the Spirit and, consequently, cannot be empowered by the Spirit. We must learn to pray the Scriptures, because in them we are taught the language of the Spirit - God's very own thoughts and desires.[48] When we know God's language we can then pray and be certain of God's answer.

> *In the same way no one knows the thoughts of God except the Spirit of God. We have not received the spirit of the world but the Spirit who is from God, that we may understand what God has freely given us. This is what*

---

47 Oepke, "agrupneo," TDNT.

48 Wesley and Stacey Campbell, *Praying the Bible: The Pathway to Spirituality* (Ventura, California: Regal Books, 2003), p. 139.

> *we speak, not in words taught us by human wisdom but in words taught by the Spirit, expressing spiritual truths in spiritual words (1 Corinthians 2: 11b – 13).*

If we are to pray with power, we must learn to pray with God's language to overcome the language of Satan, the world and the sinful nature that constantly bombard our hearts and minds. To pray the Scriptures is to pray with power.

It is time to turn off the entertainment fantasies of imaginary Hollywood heroes and live the real adventure awaiting God's chosen warriors, wielding the sword of the Spirit in the battlefield of prayer. Jesus is the Master Swordsman, the living Word (John 1:1), from whose mouth proceeds a sharp sword.

> *I saw heaven standing open and there before me was a white horse, whose rider is called Faithful and True. With justice he judges and makes war. His eyes are like blazing fire, and on his head are many crowns. He has a name written on him that no one knows but he himself. He is dressed in a robe dipped in blood, and <u>his name is the Word of God</u>. The armies of heaven were following him, riding on white horses and dressed in fine linen, white and clean. <u>Out of his mouth comes a sharp sword with which to strike down the nations</u> (Revelation 19:11-15).*

The Master Swordsman waits for us to come to him with the Word in prayer so that he may train us and prepare us to join his army. Only then will we be able to take our stand and cause the enemy to tremble.

In your battle with temptation and sin, the next time that the enemy tries to convince you to give up, remember that you are not alone in the battle. "*Therefore, since we are surrounded by such a great cloud of witnesses, let us throw off everything that hinders and the sin that so easily entangles, and let us run with perseverance the race marked out for us" (Hebrews 12:1).* There are many, like Peter and Paul, who have run the race and are cheering us on with advice and encouragement from their own lives and experience. Their advice is that we are to find our strength in Christ, who went ahead of us and suffered for us so that we could have everything we need for our race. Like Peter and Paul, we will learn the great privilege of sharing in his sufferings so that we may also share in his glorious inheritance. *"Let us fix our eyes on Jesus, the author and perfecter of our faith, who for the joy set before him endured the cross... Consider him who endured such opposition from sinful men, <u>so that you will not grow weary and lose heart</u>" (Hebrews 12:2-4).*

Questions for Reflection:

1. Have you ever experienced spiritual attack in the early morning hours? Explain.

2. What can we learn from Peter´s negligence in not heeding Jesus´ invitation to pray with him during the night watch?

3. By contrast, what can we learn about the victory of Paul and Silas praying the watch, even though the Enemy had them physically bound and imprisoned? (Acts 16:25-30)

4. Why do you think it is important to use the armor of God and, specifically, the Word of God in prayer? (Ephesians 6:10-20; 1 Corinthians 2:11b-13)

5. Have you personally or corporately used the Scriptures in prayer? Explain.

The Fourth Watch (3 a.m.)

When the military watchman (the "cock") sounded the trumpet twice at three in the morning, it was the end of the third and the beginning of the fourth and final watch (Mark 14:72). The fourth watch is the watch of supernatural revelation and kingdom breakthrough for those who have persisted in watching and praying in the spiritual realm (Psalm 130: 5-6). In the book of Exodus, we discover that Israel's breakthrough against the opposition of Pharaoh and the Egyptian army came during this watch. Pharaoh assumed that the sun god, Ra, whom he personified, would be reborn and renewed in the last watch of the night and would demonstrate his sovereignty over the Hebrew God.

The last watch is the watch of anticipation of God's power...It was near the end of this watch that all the power of God was unleashed in the resurrection of Jesus from the dead as the firstfruits of the new creation.

> *During the last watch of the night the Lord looked down from the pillar of fire and cloud at the Egyptian army and threw it into confusion. He made the wheels of their chariots come off so that they had difficulty driving. And the Egyptians said: "Let's get away from the Israelites! The Lord is fighting for them against Egypt" (Exodus 14:24-25).*

This happened in response to Moses' intercession as he remained faithful in obeying God's command to raise his staff and extend his hand over the sea (Exodus 14:16). But this was no quick intercession. The reward in the last watch came because he had persisted all night in intercession with his hand extended.

> *Then Moses stretched out his hand over the sea, and all that night the Lord drove the sea back with a strong east wind and turned it into dry land. The waters were divided, and the Israelites went through the sea on dry ground, with a wall of water on their right and on their left… Then the Lord said to Moses, "Stretch out your hand over the sea so that the waters may flow back over the Egyptians and their chariots and horsemen." Moses stretched out his hand over the sea, and at daybreak the sea went back to its place. …The water flowed back and covered the chariots and horsemen – the entire army of Pharaoh that had followed the Israelites into the sea. Not one of them survived (Exodus 14:21-22, 26-28).*

This was not the only time Moses learned the lesson of the power of persistence in intercession with outstretched hands. Only a short time after their deliverance from the Egyptians, the Israelites also defeated the Amalekite army.

> *As long as Moses held up his hands, the Israelites were winning, but whenever he lowered his hands, the Amalekites were winning. When Moses' hands grew tired, they took a stone and put it under him and he sat on it. Aaron and Hur held his hands up – one on one side, one on the other – so that his hands remained steady till sunset. So Joshua overcame the Amalekite army with the sword. Then the Lord said to Moses, "Write this on a scroll as something to be remembered and make sure that Joshua hears it, because I will completely blot out the memory of*

> *Amalek from under heaven." Moses built an altar and called it The Lord is my Banner. He said, "For hands were lifted up to the throne of the Lord. The Lord will be at war against the Amalekites from generation to generation" (Exodus 17:11-16).*

So important was the pattern of Moses' persevering intercession with outstretched hands (with the help of Aaron and Hur) that God commanded it to be recorded and remembered. Joshua overcame by the sword, but Moses, Aaron and Hur ensured the victory with uplifted hands of prayer. The battle was not merely a physical combat but, more importantly, a spiritual one. What was happening in the physical realm was the manifestation of what was occurring in the spiritual realm. It was a battle that required unity and mutual support among Moses, Aaron, and Hur to overcome the demonic forces and break through to God's resources. Today, the battle also requires unity in prayer, one encouraging the other to persevere in intercession and seek heaven's resources, symbolized by joined, uplifted hands.

Paul, under divine authority and inspiration, commands believers everywhere to spiritual battle positions as one army, unified in prayer with uplifted hands. *"I want men everywhere to lift up holy hands in prayer, without anger or disputing" (1 Timothy 2:8).* Joshua's sword would have never tasted victory had it not been for united uplifted hands. We must remember to pray for the unified intercession of God's people, uniting in the same way as Moses, Aaron and Hur, to assure triumph over the enemy. When we lift our hands together toward heaven, we are agreeing to reach into the heavenly realm and take hold of God´s hands for all the heavenly resources required for our situation. *"In your hands are strength and power to exalt and give strength to all" (1 Chronicles 29:12).* We are humbled as we realize that the hands that take hold of us are his pierced hands. *"Can a mother forget the baby at her breast and have no compassion on the child she has borne? Though she may forget, I will not forget you! See I have engraved you on the palms of my hands" (Isaiah 49:15, 16).*

The enemy will do all he can to keep us from joining our hands and hearts in united prayer. He will do it by seeking to cause disputes, division, rivalry, and mistrust. He knows that heaven's power will be unleashed against him from generation to generation by believers coming together in prayer. It is the divine trumpet call to united prayer which can cross all denominational and doctrinal boundaries. It will rally believers for the final conquest in the battle that will culminate in the Lord's return. Jesus will return to find a faithful bride, a warrior bride persevering in prayer and intercession, awaiting the arrival and intervention of her Bridegroom. But each believer must choose to be part of this end -time movement of united prayer.

An amazing event in the New Testament that demonstrates the fourth prayer watch as a breakthrough watch can be seen in Jesus' activity in Matthew 14. After having fed thousands of people (5000 men as well as thousands of women and children), Jesus sent his disciples across the lake in a boat while he went up a mountain to pray by himself. While one needs to be careful in comparing Old and New Testament events, there can be little doubt that this event was to show Jesus' superiority to Moses at the Red Sea. As with Moses, we find Jesus praying throughout the night, while the disciples struggled against the wind and the waves, wondering if they would make it to the other side. In the case of Moses, intercession and faith opened the way for God to divide the Red Sea in two, creating a pathway of dry ground for the people. However, Jesus' prayer enabled him to walk across the sea to the disciples in the last watch. *"During the fourth watch of the night Jesus went out to them, walking on the lake" (Matthew 14:25).*

This also enabled him to prompt the faith of one of the disciples, Peter, to walk with him on the water (Matthew 14:22-31). While Moses' prayer opened heaven's gates and supernatural resources for the people to get to the other side, Jesus' prayer invites each one of his disciples to participate in the supernatural with him. He wants us to experience his supernatural power and intervention in prayer. His goal is not only that we get to the other side in each test. The way in which we get to the other side must testify to his glorious power in us through prayer.

The call to fourth-watch prayer emphasizes Jesus' invitation and encouragement to participate in the supernatural with him. From the beginning to the end of his ministry on earth, it was Jesus' practice to get up and pray during the last watch, while it was still dark (Mark 1:35). The last watch is the watch of anticipation of God's power. It was these last watch times of prayer that sustained him, as he looked forward to what his Father would do during those very hours (Hebrews 12:2). It was near the end of this watch that all the power of God was unleashed in the resurrection of Jesus from the dead as the firstfruits of the new creation.

> *After the Sabbath, at dawn on the first day of the week, Mary Magdalene and the other Mary went to look at the tomb...The angel said to the women, "Do not be afraid, for I know that you are looking for Jesus, who was crucified. He is not here; he has risen" (Matthew 28:1, 5, 6).*

It was in this watch that the power of the resurrection was forever set in motion in Christ, and in those who are in him. *"And if the Spirit of him who raised Jesus from the dead is living in you, he who raised Christ from the dead will also give life to your mortal bodies through his Spirit, who lives in you" (Romans 8:11).*

The power of the resurrection in Christ Jesus, through the Holy Spirit, has now been activated in us. We will not experience the fullness of its power until the Second Coming of Christ. But right now, we can experience its power if we will get rid of the limitations that have hindered our faith in the resurrected Christ. In the same way that Jesus challenged the limitations of Martha´s faith in him, he challenges us: *"Take away the stone…Did I not tell you that if you believed, you would see the glory of God?" (John 11:39-41).* It is time to pray and persevere in our faith, taking away the stone of our self-imposed human limitations. It is time to let loose the power of the resurrection that is in us, in the same way that Lazarus was let loose from the grave clothes that bound him (John 11:44). We need to pray, expecting the release of resurrection power in all the areas in which we have been battling in intercession.

As we pray in the power of the resurrection, we need to pray for Christ's return. We need to remember that the full power of the resurrection to transform our bodies and even the earth itself will only be realized upon the return of Christ. When he appears, we will appear with him in our transformed glorified bodies (Colossians 3:4). Not only the Church, but also creation is awaiting that moment when it too will be set free from the horrible affects of corruption, contamination and death that resulted from the fall of humanity. Just as creation was horribly marred by our sin and corruption, so too she awaits the restoration to her pristine condition the day Christ's transforming work is completed in us. *"Against its will, all creation was subjected to God's curse. But with eager hope, the creation looks forward to the day when it will join God's children in glorious freedom from death and decay" (Romans 8:20, 21 NLT).* Since all of creation has put its hope in our transformation, we need to keep our hope fully set on the One who promises on his return to bring to completion the good work he began in us (Philippians 1:6). Our full reward is not now, but when he comes. With this prayer perspective, the early believers' prayer cry was *"Maranatha! Our Lord, come!" (1 Corinthians 16:22; Revelation 22:20; Good News Translation)*. We are to be instruments of the kingdom of heaven's reign on earth, as a kingdom of priests. But the full realization of Christ's reign will not be manifested until he is revealed in power and majesty at his Second Coming.

Questions for Reflection:

1. Have you ever had "revelatory" experiences of Christ´s presence during the last watch (between 3 and 6 a.m.)? If so, describe your experience.

2. The fourth watch is characterized by waiting and persevering prayer. Why do you think God requires us to wait or persevere in prayer before he responds and reveals his power? (See Psalm 130: 5,6)

3. Why do you think Jesus first revealed his resurrection power to the women among his followers? (Read Matthew 28:1-10)

4. How does Romans 8:11 motivate you to seek and experience his resurrection power in your life now? How does it give you hope for the future?

VI. The Divine Prayer Clock In Church History

The body of Christ, the kingdom of priests, has been seated with him at the highest level of spiritual authority in the universe (Ephesians 1:22, 2:6). This has been achieved through his resurrection and ascension. As Paul Billheimer states:

> Redeemed humanity outranks all other orders of created beings in the universe...Through the use of her weapons of prayer and faith, she holds in this present throbbing moment the balance of power in world affairs...the mightiest force for civilization and enlightened social consciousness in the world today...the only force contesting Satan's total rule in human affairs.[49]

Through the divine prayer clock, he has revealed to us a plan for a 24/7 prayer lifestyle by which his work on Calvary can be understood and activated around the globe.

Christ went to the cross with his bride in sight, redeemed to rule beside him. It is a kingdom of interceding and worshiping priests that will extend his redemption and reign across the globe and throughout the universe.

For Christ's body to extend his redemption and

---

49 Paul Billheimer, *Destined for the Throne* (Minneapolis, Minnesota: Bethany House Publishers, 1975), pp. 15, 16.

rule throughout all of creation, she must first understand her existence in terms of his redemption and rule. Time can no longer be seen as merely an agenda to be filled with endless activity. It is Satan's strategy to occupy our lives with "chronos" time, keeping us from fulfilling our divine destiny to rule with Christ. However, rather than having our lives consumed by "chronos", Christ calls us to see time from God's divine "kairos" calendar. Instead of being consumed by meaningless activity, he has called us to a place of rest where we can be restored to the eternal meaning and purpose for which we were created. Christ desires to transform our present rhythm of life with its busy schedules to a rhythm of spiritual rest, renewal and rule through prayer. Then we will learn how to become instruments of redemption. He wants to reveal to us the secret of David's incredibly influential life, that flowed from a rhythm of prayer which informed and empowered his day and activity. David's day and night were structured around seven times of prayer and worship. It was that spiritual structure that enabled him to live with a constant awareness of God's sovereign presence and direction (Psalm 119:164). It was a discovery that probably influenced David's plan to organize the priesthood and the nation to adopt a rhythm of continual prayer through a simple tabernacle – the tabernacle of David.

Then God made a covenant with David promising him that one of his sons would build the house that he wanted. His throne would endure forever (1 Chronicles 17:11-14). It is Jesus who is overseeing the building of that house, the rebuilt tabernacle of David. It is no longer a physical place but a spiritual place in which God's presence dwells, and where those who believe in him can dwell and rule with him through prayer. It is called the house of prayer (Mark 11:17). In the house of prayer, our time is no longer to be perceived as a busy agenda, but rather as an opportunity to live in God's presence with eternal purpose and destiny. This is reflected in a divine prayer clock, in which each hour of prayer is redeemed and given its meaning and purpose in the crucifixion and resurrection of Christ. It is a divine clock in which God's eternal purposes in Christ, the Alpha and Omega, are being restored to a human existence that is running out of time and hope.

God has set before us two amazing promises to bring about the transformation of the world in which we live. First, if we will redeem our activity by participating in the building of the spiritual house of prayer, as living stones, the rest of humanity will seek Christ (Acts 15:16–18). Second, if we will redeem our time with his prayer clock and begin to truly function as a kingdom of priests in 24/7 intercession, Christ's rule will extend around the globe (Revelation 5:9, 10). We must apply Christ's redemption to both our time and our activity if his redemption and rule are to extend through us to the rest of the world. Paul Billheimer defines our call to prayer:

> It is implementing upon earth Heaven's decisions concerning the affairs of men. Calvary legally destroyed Satan, and canceled all of his claims. God placed the enforcement of Calvary's victory in the hands of the Church. He has given her "power of attorney." She is his "deputy." But this delegated authority is wholly inoperative apart from the prayers of a believing Church. Therefore, prayer is where the action is. Any church without a well-organized and systematic prayer program is simply operating a religious treadmill.[50]

I believe Christ has revealed in the Scriptures much more than a program of systematic prayer.

---

50 Paul Billheimer, pp. 17-18.

Through the divine prayer clock, he has revealed to us a plan for a 24/7 prayer lifestyle by which his work on Calvary can be understood and activated around the globe. It is a plan that equips us as a kingdom of redeemed priests to extend and apply the work of Christ through prayer to the Church (hour of incense), to the nations and their governments (sixth hour), to the next generations (first watch), and to the world's future (fourth watch). It is a plan that empowers us with the Holy Spirit (third hour) and enables us to prepare spiritually (second watch) to defeat Satan, the world and the sin nature (third watch). It is a plan that reminds us of our direct access to Christ's throne (ninth hour) and can revolutionize our lives, our church and our world. But, it comes down to a single decision. Will we continue to perceive time and life as mere activity, influenced by people and circumstances? Or will we let our time and life be redeemed by Christ so that we can influence people and circumstances through prayer? What have Christians in other centuries decided? What can we learn from them? Is there evidence that the prayer clock influenced Christians in the centuries following Christ and the early church?

Late in the second century, a prominent leader of the church named Tertullian (c. 160–225 AD) recorded the practice of Christian prayer to be as follows: after sunrise (morning hour of incense); third hour; sixth hour; ninth hour; before sunset (first watch); after dark (second watch).[51] This is confirmed in the writings of other outstanding Christian contemporaries of Tertullian, such as Clement (c. 150–215 AD) and Origen (c. 185–254 AD).[52] In reality, Christianity at the time of Tertullian (only 200 years after Christ) appeared to practise

---

51 Jo Ellen Burnett, *Time Pendulum* (New York: Plenum Press, 1998), p. 45.

52 Phyllis Tickle, p. xi.

all of the prayer hours identified in the Scriptures, except the last two watches. Christians at the time of Tertullian had decided that their lives would be informed and directed by a spiritual life rhythm, not a worldly rhythm. While the hours of the clock were secular time points for the Roman military, government, business, and the general populace, for the Christians they had divine significance, transformed by Christ in prayer.

The desert fathers, the earliest monastics of the Church (3rd century), sought to live out Paul's admonition to *"pray without ceasing" (1 Thessalonians 5:17, KJV)*. They accomplished this through a prayer relay, whereby one group of intercessors passed the torch of prayer on to the next, to ensure that the prayer torch was never dropped. The goal was to ensure that there were always intercessors of their Christian community before the throne of God.[53]

At the time of Saint Benedict (480 – 543 AD), his spiritual order was practising the following prayer cycle: laud (dawn or last watch), prime (morning hour of incense), terce (third hour), sext (sixth hour), nones (ninth hour), vespers (eleventh hour), compline (first watch), matins (night watches).[54] It appears that in Benedict's time, his order was practising the complete prayer clock and, in addition, added the eleventh hour. The times were divided between individual and group prayer, but always with the community in mind. No one wanted to be late or miss prayer because they did not want to be disconnected from the spiritual rhythm of life in Christ experienced through prayer. Consequently, mechanical clocks were developed by blacksmiths to help monks arrive on time. It is interesting to note that the first mechanical clocks were developed with prayer

---

53 Ibid.

54 Jo Ellen Burnett, pp. 45 – 47.

in mind, not business.[55] Time and life were to be conceived as an opportunity to offer oneself as a gift in worship to God, rather than merely passing the days.[56] "The prayer clock was meant to be a guide for a communal life of humility and obedience in devotion to God."[57] It meant "renouncing the pursuit of self interest, personal property, and personal control of one's time…in a gradual preparation for life in the hereafter."[58]

In the fourteenth and fifteenth centuries, the faithful stopped and prayed wherever they were when they heard the church bells ring. The bells called them to pray at the designated hours.[59] It was also common for the intercessors to carry a "Book of Hours" with specific prayers, among which were the prayers marking the hours of the crucifixion of Christ and the work of the Holy Spirit.[60]

The Moravians are an amazing example of what can happen when a group of believers decide to allow Christ to redeem and rule their time and lives through the prayer clock. The community of believers that had gathered from various denominations and backgrounds to meet on Count Zinzendorf's property began as a divisive and conflictive group. Then Count Zinzendorf, along with a few others, covenanted to pray for revival. On the May 12, 1727, revival came and

---

55 David Christianson, *Timepieces* (Toronto: Firefly Books, 2002), p. 21.

56 Jo Ellen Burnett, p. 47.

57 Gerhard Dohrn-van Rossum, *The History of the Hour* (Chicago: University of Chicago Press, 1996), p. 35.

58 Ibid.

59 Paul F. Bradshaw, "Bells and The Liturgy of Hours," *The New SCM Dictionary of Liturgy and Worship* (London, England: SCM Press, 2002), p 57.

60 Victor Leroquais, *Les Livres d' Heures* (Paris: Manuscrits de la Biblioteque Nacionale, 1927), p. XXVI.

Zinzendorf commented that: "The whole place represented truly and visibly the habitation of God among men."[61] Zinzendorf had stumbled upon the house of prayer, the rebuilt tabernacle of David. On August 27, 1727, as a result of Zinzendorf's prayer covenant and the subsequent revival, twenty-four men and twenty-four women covenanted to pray one hour each day to assure nonstop prayer around the clock. It was a prayer clock movement of continual, 24/7 prayer that would last for over one hundred years. [62]

In 1791, sixty-five years after the commencement of the prayer vigil, this small prayer movement had sent out their 300th missionary from their group of intercessors.[63] It is well-documented that the Moravians sent out missionaries to the most difficult mission fields around the world, reaching the Virgin Islands, Greenland, Surinam, the Gold Coast, North America and South Africa by 1740 – only thirteen years after their prayer covenant.[64] Their compassion and sacrificial commitment to evangelization are unparalleled in the history of missions. At least one historian has estimated that the Moravians achieved more in missions in this period than all of the Protestant efforts before them.[65] An English Moravian named James Hutton was to play a leading role in the English Revival. Other Moravians, among them Peter Bohler, were used of God in John

---

61 Leslick Tann, "A Prayer Meeting That Lasted 100 Years," Church History, Issue 1, 1982, www.etlibrary.com/ch/1982/issue_(accessed 16 April, 2009).

62 Ibid.

63 Ibid.

64 James De Jong, "Expansion World-Wide," *The History of Christianity* (Oxford, England: Lion Hudson, 1996), p. 482.

65 Ibid.

Wesley's conversion and anointing by the Holy Spirit.[66] Wesley would be a significant figure in the growth and expansion of the English Revival because of the Moravians. The decision of Zinzendorf and the Moravian believers to covenant to pray continuously and systematically had a far-reaching impact. There can be no doubt that revival, missions and continuous 24/7 prayer were inseparable partners.

Wherever God's kingdom is advancing in a significant way, there is certain to be a group of believers who have rediscovered the house of prayer, with its 24/7 prayer clock. Even in contemporary church history, there are amazing examples. One that hits close to home is Cuba. God's move began with an unknown pastor named Juan who was agonizing in prayer and fasting in his little church building. He was pounding at heaven's doors for revival in Cuba. God's response came on a Tuesday morning in 1987. As Juan prayed, God began to reveal to him a map of Cuba with a cross passing over it, back and forth, inscribing into the land the words: CUBA PARA CRISTO...Cuba for Christ! Pastor Juan was so excited about the vision that he began to share it with his friends. Soon people came to pray according to the vision, and decided to organize themselves to pray 24 hours a day, 7 days a week, with different teams praying every half hour. Then Pastor Juan traveled across the nation sharing the vision and the call to prayer. By the end of 1988, the 24/7 prayer had spread to 100,000 Christians in local churches across the nation.[67] The prayer movement crossed all denominational boundaries. The body of Christ in Cuba had

---

66 A. Skevington Wood, "Awakening," *The History of Christianity,* p. 446.

67 Hermano Pablo and Brother Andrew, *Cuba Para Cristo: The Amazing Story of Revival in Cuba* (Canada: Open Doors, 1998), p. 5.

responded to the Master's call to restore the house of prayer, and to extend his rule as a united royal priesthood. Their lives were now being directed by his divine schedule and clock.

The revival began in 1988 after almost a year of continuous prayer. It began in a little rural town called Madruga, just outside of the capital city of Havana. People were lining up at two in the morning to get into the prayer meetings. As soon as people entered the building, they would begin to weep in response to the powerful presence of holiness. God's glory was there. It was not long until the first miracles and instant healings took place. After the main services, the pastoral staff often counselled over 300 people for conversion. In six months, over 100,000 people passed through the doors of a sanctuary that normally sat 300.[68] Soon the news spread that God had also shown up in another church and then another, of every denomination. The signs were the same: a powerful sense of holiness, repentance, conversions, healings and miracles. The greatest sign was the desire to pray. The sanctuaries would fill hours before the services as people came and knelt and prayed. The overflow of people praying carried onto the streets.[69] By the end of 1991, the revival had generated more than 2400 house churches. The revival spawned a house church movement that accounts for the majority of Cuban believers that meet to worship Christ today.

However, as one Cuban pastor recently explained to me: "With the growth and organization, we forgot something, the most important thing – prayer." Another Christian leader recalled the change that halted the revival: "Somewhere along the way, the pre-service prayer, the sense of holiness as the congregations prepared to meet with God on their knees, was re-

---

68 Ibid., p. 6.

69 Ibid., p. 9.

placed by pre-service social time and conversation. The sense of holiness – of anticipating God's presence - was lost." However, as both of these men reflected on the scriptural revelation concerning the divine prayer clock, their response was the same: "This is what we had forgotten!"

It has been exciting to watch more than 1400 pastors and leaders from more than thirty denominations unite, together with their congregations, to pray the prayer clock.The cell phone has been particularly useful in organizing the movement in Cuba. When the cell phone rings two times, the agreed upon prayer code, and the name of the prayer partner appears on the screen, each one stops to pray wherever they are. In Cuba, it is no longer church bells but cell phones that are instrumental in calling believers to prayer. Times have changed, but the call to prayer has not.

It is not God who stops revival. It stops when God's people forget to function as a kingdom of priests, restoring the house of prayer, guided by his divine schedule and clock. I believe that the discovery in the Scriptures concerning a divine prayer clock is a wake-up call, not only to the Cuban believers, but to all believers. If we as his children will unite to seek him, the rest of humanity will also seek him (Acts 15:16, 17). In reality, it is the only thing holding back the transformation of this world. One thing he asks of us: that we unite in continual prayer. If we do that, the rest of humanity will begin seeking God and the hearts of men and women of all ages, nations, languages and cultures will become fertile ground for us to share the good news of Christ. The ground is hard because it has not been plowed by the united prayer of the saints. There is a world revival that awaits us before the Second Coming of Christ. It will take place as we rebuild the tabernacle of David with united, continuous prayer. That is the house God awaits.

The kingdom of Christ will be extended and administered in this world by you, me and every other believer who will pray and intercede together according to his plan.

> *"You are worthy to take the scroll and to open its seals, because you were slain and with your blood you purchased men for God from every tribe and language, people and nation. You have made them to be a kingdom and priests to serve our God, and they will reign on the earth" (Revelation 5:9, 10).*

Christ paid a high price to redeem us for this purpose. As his house of prayer, it is time to become organized in such a way as to assure that the 24-hour prayer times are covered in the day and the night. I am recommending that each Christian in a local church choose one hour daily in the prayer clock, during the day or in the night watches, to pray as part of a corporate prayer chain. If Jesus expected that of his disciples, like Peter, it is unlikely that his expectations have changed for his disciples in our time (Matthew 26:40, 42). As we do so, we will be synchronizing our prayers on earth with the living creatures and the 24 elders who are in heaven before the throne 24/7 (Revelation 4:6-11). They represent the full will of God's kingdom plan for his creation and his people. Then we will see his kingdom come and his will become fully active on earth as it is in heaven.

Now that you have read and meditated on this divine prayer plan revealed to us in the Scriptures, and practised throughout church history, it is my prayer that you will take it and join us in following Christ to rebuild the House of Prayer for all nations.

Questions for Reflection:

1. If, as Paul Billheimer believes, praying Christians are "the mightiest force for civilization and enlightened social consciousness in the world today", why are so few Christians and local churches praying passionately?

2. What can be done to awaken the church from Satan´s strategy of meaningless "chronos" activity to discover her "kairos" destiny as a 24/7 kingdom of priests?

3. There have been many significant movements to rebuild the 24/7 House of Prayer. Do you believe you and your local church are ready to be part of a last day's movement to rebuild the 24/7 House of Prayer called "David´s tabernacle"? Why or why not?

4. What are you willing to do in order to see you and your church´s participation become a reality?

VII. A 24-Hour Prayer Plan

As you seek to be part of Christ's plan to rebuild the house of continuous prayer, remember that it is a process. It will not be built in a day. The enemy has been at work, as in the days of Ezra and Nehemiah, to discourage the rebuilding of the temple and the walls of Jerusalem. Zerubbabel was appointed to supervise the rebuilding of the temple, and one by one had to deal with the enemies´ strategies.

As you personally begin to use this manual and to teach and encourage others to form a network of 24/7 prayer, remember to begin when and where people are available.

First, the enemy offered to help in the building so that he could deviate the work from God's instructions and water it down with his own plan (Ezra 4:1-3). Today's Christianity must confront the same strategy. The enemy has convinced believers that the house of God should be based upon a design of polished organization and programs rather than prayer. Rather than being a model for transformation, demonstrating a kingdom lifestyle, we have modelled the latest marketing techniques to sell the message. The results have been just as the enemy expected. Zerubbabel refused to allow the enemy to participate in the building (Ezra 3:3). Today God is raising up a movement of 24-hour prayer networks of believers around the globe.[70] They refuse to be side-tracked from following Christ in restoring the divine design for the House of God – a House of Prayer for all nations (Mark 11:17). The movement is gathering force.

Second, the enemy identified opponents from within God's own people. These individuals focused more on their personal interests than on God's kingdom. Satan used them to influence and hinder the rebuilding from within (Ezra 4:4). In the same way, there will be those of the congregation who will oppose and influence others to resist the plan. The words and plans of the opponents in Zerubbabel's time were overcome by God's prophetic word through the prophets (Ezra 5:1,2). So too, God will give his word and anointing to birth a vision in your church and community that will not be stopped. God will move in the hearts of his people and leadership, possibly to the levels of civil government (Ezra 6).

In the province in which my wife and I live, the provincial government has invited a prayer network of Christians called SHOP (Saskatchewan House of Prayer) to pray regularly in the provincial government legislature buildings in Regina, Saskatchewan. They were assigned a board room opposite the Speaker of the House for prayer.[71] We are entering an exciting time for the church as believers begin to awaken to the power and authority that Christ has placed in their hands and hearts through prayer. In Latin America, we are seeing the believers being awakened to this reality. Those who persevere will be part of the greatest spiritual move in the history of the church.

---

70 Pete Greig and Dave Roberts, *Red Moon Rising* (Orlando, Florida: Relevant Books, 2005), pp. 244-245.

71 Richard Lepp, "Government Gate" (May 2008), www.saskatchewanhouseofprayer.org, (accessed 23 December, 2008).

As you personally begin to use this manual to teach and encourage others to form a network of 24/7 prayer, remember to begin when and where people are available. With time and patience, God will place in the hearts of his people the passion to pray during the watches that are most vital and yet most difficult. The watches of the early morning hours are essential, and were emphasized by Jesus as most important (Luke 12:37, 38). Initially, they will be the most difficult for which to find intercessors, until some discover just how much God reveals himself during those hours. Where more grace is needed, more grace is given. Remember the principle that, as we sacrifice time and energy to offer our incense of prayer, God will add what is lacking (Revelation 8:3, 4). He will give us all we need and more to motivate and stir us to pray in the most difficult and challenging hours.

This manual is to be used in a way that works best for your network. It is designed upon the assumption that each intercessor will choose one hour daily to pray as part of a 24-hour united prayer plan. Each prayer shift, whether in the day or night, is assigned three prayer motives for the three hours of the prayer watch or shift. All of the prayer motives can be prayed together in the hour chosen by the intercessor. Or, the intercessor can focus on one prayer motive but go into significant depth and detail, as led by the Spirit. Whatever the case, they are not meant to be a rule. They are a guide for praying according to the specific prayer theme of the prayer watch. In that way, you can be sensitive to the Holy Spirit's promptings as you pray. Use the prophetic Scriptures given to you in the prayer guide. The Scriptures have been supplied with the prayer themes so that they can be read, meditated upon, and then used in your prayers. Listen to the Spirit as he directs you to other Scriptures as well.

You probably noted that, in the first part of this manual, there was a diagram for each prayer time of the divine prayer clock. These illustrations are memory devices to help the intercessor remember the content and motives of the hours of prayer. In the final pages of the manual, you will encounter the prayer clock diagram. This can be a useful tool as you begin to organize in order to cover the prayer times. You can do this by creating a prayer clock on which intercessors will be able to write their names in the prayer hours or watches to which they are committing. One of the keys to maintaining the excitement as a prayer movement is to designate someone for each watch or hour to ring the others by phone at the beginning of the prayer hour. It is a reminder that you are not alone in your intercession. A code of two rings could be set as the prayer signal. Remember, the goal of the prayer clock is to help you develop a spiritual rhythm for your life. So even though you may have finished praying the hour to which you committed as a part of the local Christian community, you can still practise the prayer clock throughout the rest of the day. This can be done by taking a few moments of reflection and prayer as you look at your watch, and are reminded of the spiritual significance of that hour.

Once again, remember, this is a process. The foundation must be well-laid before the rest of the structure will rise. The Lord's advice to Zerubbabel and the people of Judah in laying the foundation for the rebuilding of the temple was: *"Do not despise these small beginnings, for the Lord rejoices to see the work begin, to see the plumb line in Zerubbabel's hand" (Zechariah 4:10).*[72] As you begin, remember that the Lord is rejoicing, having put the plumb line of prayer into your hands

---

72 *New Living Version.*

so that his house is rebuilt exactly according to his design. As you do so, you will be joining hundreds of thousands around the world who have been called by the Master Carpenter and Builder, Jesus Christ, to join him in building the House that his Father and our Father wants. *"My Father's house shall be called a house of prayer for all nations"(Mark 11:17; Isaiah 56:7).*

Questions for Reflection:

1. The key to launching a 24/7 movement of prayer is to identify intercessors in your church who will work with you on a team. Who are some of the prayer warriors in your church?

2. Your congregation will probably not be able to immediately cover a 24/7 prayer schedule. Which other congregations might be candidates for networking with your church in a 24/7 prayer network? Remember, the greater the participation and unity in the body of Christ, the greater the impact.

3. Prepare yourself for counter-attacks from the enemy as you approach the front lines of spiritual battle. What are some of the ways that the enemy might try to discourage you?

4. Remember the key to success will be your own obedience and testimony as part of the 24/7 House of Prayer. Who is someone with whom you feel you can be open and accountable in order to keep you on track?

Morning Hour Of Incense: 6 a.m.

Theme: God´s People

Prayer Guide:

1. Pray for grace to hear and to obey God's voice from his Word.
2. Pray for God's people (in your life and church) by name as precious living stones.
3. Pray for God to raise up others to join you in the kingdom of priests, as a 24-hour prayer network, bringing the incense of prayer before his throne.

Scripture:

"Now if you obey me fully and keep my covenant, then out of all the nations you will be my treasured possession. Although the whole earth is mine, you will be for me a kingdom of priests and a holy nation" (Exodus 19:4-6).

"This is what you are to offer on the altar regularly each day: two lambs a year old. Offer one in the morning and the other at twilight...For the generations to come this burnt offering is to be made regularly at the entrance to the Tent of Meeting before the Lord. There I will meet you and speak to you; and the place will be consecrated by my glory" (Exodus 29:38-39, 42-43).

"Aaron must burn fragrant incense on the altar every morning when he tends the lamps. He must burn incense again when he lights the lamps at twilight, so incense will burn regularly before the Lord for the generations to come" (Exodus 30:7,8).

"There are to be twelve stones, one for each of the names

of the sons of Israel, each engraved like a seal with the name of one of the twelve tribes...Whenever Aaron enters the Holy Place, he will bear the names of the sons of Israel over his heart on the breastpiece of decision as a continuing memorial before the Lord" (Exodus 28:21, 29).

"And when <u>the time for the burning of incense</u> came, all the assembled worshipers were praying outside" (Luke 1:10).

"As you come to him, the living Stone – rejected by men but chosen by God and precious to him – you also, like living stones, are being built into a spiritual house to be a holy priesthood, offering spiritual sacrifices acceptable to God through Jesus Christ"(1 Peter 2:4,5).

"May my prayer be set before you like incense; may the lifting up of my hands be like the evening sacrifice" (Psalm 141:2).

"And when he had taken it, the four living creatures and the twenty-four elders fell down before the Lamb. Each one had a harp and they were holding golden bowls full of incense, which are the prayers of the saints" (Revelation 5:8).

"Another angel, who had a golden censer, came and stood at the altar. He was given much incense to offer, with the prayers of the all the saints, on the golden altar before the throne. The smoke of the incense, together with the prayers of the saints, went up before God from the angel's hand" (Revelation 8:3-5).

" 'My name will be great among the nations, from the rising to the setting of the sun. In every place incense and pure offerings will be brought to my name, because my name will be great among the nations,' says the Lord Almighty" (Malachi 1:11).

Third Hour Of Prayer: 9 a.m.

Theme: Anointing of the Holy Spirit

Prayer Guide:

1. Wait in prayer and worship, asking for and receiving in faith the anointing and filling of the Holy Spirit.

2. Intercede for the body of Christ asking for the priestly anointing of forgiveness and reconciliation to be renewed in and through the church.

3. Intercede for the body of Christ asking for the kingdom anointing so that the good news of forgiveness in Christ will be accompanied by the power of Christ.

Scripture:

"It was the third hour when they crucified him" (Mark 15:25).

"Then he opened their minds so they could understand the Scriptures. He told them, 'This is what is written: The Christ will suffer and rise from the dead on the third day, and repentance and forgiveness of sins will be preached in his name to all nations, beginning at Jerusalem. You are witnesses of these things. I am going to send you what my Father has promised; but stay in the city until you have been clothed with power from on high' " (Luke 24:45-49).

"Again Jesus said: 'Peace be with you! As the Father has sent me, I am sending you.' And with that he breathed on them and said, 'Receive the Holy Spirit. If you forgive anyone his sins, they are forgiven; if you do not forgive them, they are not forgiven' " (John 20:21-23).

"They all joined together constantly in prayer, along with the women and Mary the mother of Jesus, and with his brothers...When the day of Pentecost came, they were all together in one place. Suddenly a sound like a blowing of a violent wind came from heaven and filled the whole house where they were sitting. They saw what seemed to be tongues of fire that separated and came to rest on each of them. All of them were filled with the Holy Spirit and began to speak in other tongues as the Spirit enabled them... Then Peter stood up with the Eleven, raised his voice and addressed the crowd: 'Fellow Jews and all of you who live in Jerusalem, let me explain this to you; listen carefully to what I say. These men are not drunk, as you suppose. It's only nine in the morning. No, this is what was spoken by the prophet Joel' "(Acts 1:14; 2:1-4; 2:14-16).

"God has raised this Jesus to life, and we are all witnesses of the fact. Exalted to the right hand of God, he has received from the Father the promised Holy Spirit and has poured out what you now see and hear...Therefore let all Israel be assured of this: God has made this Jesus, whom you crucified, both Lord and Christ" (Acts 2:32-33, 36).

" 'Now, Lord, consider their threats and enable your servants to speak your word with great boldness. Stretch out your hand to heal and perform miraculous signs and wonders through the name of your holy servant Jesus.' After they prayed, the place where they were meeting was shaken. And they were all filled with the Holy Spirit and spoke the word of God boldly" (Acts 4:29-31).

"So I say to you: ask and it will be given to you; seek and you will find; knock and the door will be opened to you.... If you then, though you are evil, know how to give good

gifts to your children, how much more will your Father in heaven give the Holy Spirit to those who ask him!" (Luke 11:9-10, 13).

"Do not get drunk on wine… Instead, be filled with the Spirit. Speak to one another with psalms, hymns and spiritual songs. Sing and make music in your heart to the Lord, always giving thanks to God the Father for everything, in the name of our Lord Jesus Christ. Submit to one another out of reverence for Christ" (Ephesians 5:18-21).

Sixth Hour Of Prayer: 12 Noon

Theme: The Nations

Prayer Guide:

1. Pray that the light of the Gospel of Jesus Christ push back the darkness and the spiritual blindness evident in our nation.

2. Intercede for the spiritual harvest of the nations (choose several nations that you have been reading about or have a special interest in). Remember to pray for their rulers and governments to be open to the Gospel.

3. Pray that the Lord of the harvest send workers with spiritual authority to these nations. Be ready to answer his call on your life.

Scripture:

"From the sixth hour until the ninth hour darkness came over all the land. About the ninth hour Jesus cried out in a loud voice, 'Eloi, Eloi, lama sabachthani?' – which means, 'My God, my God, why have you forsaken me?' " (Matthew 27:45-46).

"Yet I am writing you a new command; its truth is seen in him and you, because the darkness is passing and the true light is already shining" (1 John 2:8).

"About noon the following day as they were on their journey and approaching the city, Peter went up on the roof to pray. He became hungry and wanted something to eat, and while the meal was being prepared, he fell into

a trance. He saw heaven opened and something like a large sheet being let down to earth by its four corners. It contained all kinds of four-footed animals, as well as reptiles of the earth and birds of the air. Then a voice told him, 'Get up, Peter. Kill and eat.' ...While Peter was still thinking about the vision, the Spirit said to him, 'Simon, three men are looking for you. So get up and go downstairs. Do not hesitate to go with them, for I have sent them.' Peter went down and said to the men, 'I am the one you're looking for. Why have you come?' The men replied, 'We have come from Cornelius the centurion.' " (Acts 10:9-13,19-22).

"Now he had to go through Samaria. So he came to a town in Samaria called Sychar, near the plot of ground Jacob had given to his son Joseph. Jacob's well was there, and Jesus, tired as he was from the journey, sat down by the well. <u>It was about the sixth hour.</u> When a Samaritan woman came to draw water, Jesus said to her, 'Will you give me a drink?'...The Samaritan woman said to him, 'You are a Jew and I am a Samaritan woman. How can you ask me for a drink?'...Jesus answered her, 'If you knew the gift of God and who it is that asks you for a drink, you would have asked him and he would have given you living water'"(John 4:4-10).

" My food," said Jesus, "is to do the will of him who sent me and to finish his work. Do you not say, 'Four months more and then the harvest?' I tell you, open your eyes and look at the fields! They are ripe for the harvest." (John 4:34, 35).

"When he saw the crowds, he had compassion on them, because they were harassed and helpless, like sheep without a shepherd. Then he said to his disciples, 'The harvest is plentiful but the workers are few. Ask the Lord of the harvest, therefore, to send out workers into his harvest

field.' He called his twelve disciples to him and gave them authority to drive out evil spirits and to heal every disease and sickness" (Matthew 9:36-10:1).

"Then Jesus came to them and said, 'All authority in heaven and on earth has been given to me. Therefore go and make disciples of all nations, baptizing them in the name of the Father and of the Son and of the Holy Spirit, and teaching them to obey everything I have commanded you. And surely I am with you always, to the very end of the age'"(Matthew 28:18-20).

"I urge, then, first of all, that requests, prayers, intercession and thanksgiving be made for everyone – for kings and all those in authority, that we may live peaceful and quiet lives in all godliness and holiness. This is good, and pleases God our Savior, who wants all men to be saved and to come to knowledge of the truth" (1 Timothy 2:1-4).

Ninth Hour Of Prayer: 3 p.m.

Theme: The Throne of Grace

Prayer Guide:

1. Prayer of thanksgiving for the torn veil and direct access to the throne of grace through the sacrifice of Christ Jesus.

2. Pray for family, friends and acquaintances that have not yet come to the throne of grace.

3. Pray to be an agent of Christ's justice in acts of forgiveness, healing and love to those in need around you (church, family, community).

Scripture:

"About the ninth hour Jesus cried out in a loud voice, 'Eloi, Eloi, lama sabacthani?' – which means, 'My God, my God, why have you forsaken me?' When some of those standing there heard this, they said, 'He's calling Elijah.' Immediately one of them ran and got a sponge. He filled it with wine vinegar, put it on a stick, and offered it to Jesus to drink. The rest said, 'Now leave him alone. Let's see if Elijah comes to save him.' And when Jesus had cried out again in a loud voice, he gave up his spirit. At that moment the curtain of the temple was torn in two from top to bottom" (Matthew 27:46-51).

"Therefore, brothers, since we have confidence to enter the Most Holy Place by the blood of Jesus, by a new and living way opened for us through the curtain, that is, his body, and since we have a great priest over the house of God, let us draw near to God with a sincere heart in full assurance of faith, having our hearts sprinkled to cleanse us from a

guilty conscience and having our bodies washed with pure water" (Hebrews 10:19-22).

"Forgive us our debts, as we also have forgiven our debtors" (Matthew 6:12).

"Jesus answered, 'I am the way and the truth and the life. No one comes to the Father except through me' " (John 14:6).

"Therefore, since we have a great high priest who has gone through the heavens, Jesus the Son of God, let us hold firmly to the faith we profess. For we do not have a high priest who is unable to sympathize with our weaknesses, but we have one who has been tempted in every way, just as we are – yet was without sin. Let us then approach the throne of grace with confidence, so that we may receive mercy and find grace to help us in our time of need" (Hebrews 4:14-16).

"One day Peter and John were going up to the temple at <u>the time of prayer – at three in the afternoon.</u> Now a man crippled from birth was being carried to the temple gate called Beautiful, where he was put every day to beg from those going into the temple courts. When he saw Peter and John about to enter, he asked them for money. Peter looked straight at him, as did John. Then Peter said, 'Look at us!' So the man gave them his attention, expecting to get something from them. Then Peter said, 'Silver or gold I do not have, but what I have I give you. In the name of Jesus Christ of Nazareth, walk.' Taking him by the right hand, he helped him up, and instantly the man's feet and ankles became strong. He jumped to his feet and began to walk" (Acts 3: 1-6).

"At Caesarea there was a man named Cornelius, a centurion in what was known as the Italian Regiment. He and all his family were devout and God-fearing; he gave generously to those in need and prayed to God regularly. <u>One day at about three in the afternoon he had a vision</u>. He distinctly saw an angel of God who came to him and said, 'Cornelius!' Cornelius stared at him in fear. 'What is it, Lord?' he asked. The angel answered, 'Your prayers and gifts to the poor have come up as a memorial offering before God. Now send men to Joppa to bring back a man named Simon who is called Peter. He is staying with Simon the tanner, whose house is by the sea' "(Acts 10:1-6).

"When you spread out your hands in prayer, I will hide my eyes from you; even if you offer many prayers, I will not listen. Your hands are full of blood; wash and make yourselves clean. Take your evil deeds out of my sight! Stop doing wrong, learn to do right! Seek justice, encourage the oppressed. Defend the cause of the fatherless, plead the case of the widow. 'Come now, let us reason together,' says the Lord. 'Though your sins are like scarlet they shall be as white as snow; though they are red as crimson, they shall be like wool' " (Isaiah 1:15-18).

"And God raised us up with Christ and seated us with him in the heavenly realms in Christ Jesus...For it is by grace you have been saved, through faith – and this not of yourselves, it is the gift of God – not by works, so that no one can boast. For we are God´s workmanship, created in Christ Jesus to do good works, which God prepared in advance for us to do" (Ephesians 2:6, 8-10).

First Prayer Watch: 6 p.m.

Theme: The Children

Prayer Guide:

1. Intercede for your physical children and any other children that the Holy Spirit brings to mind.
2. Intercede for the spiritual children – the new believers in your life and in your church.
3. Pray for reconciliation in your relationship with your children (physical or spiritual), and for reconciliation between the generations in your church, community, and nation.

Scripture:

"Arise, cry out in the night, as the watches of the night begin; pour out your heart like water in the presence of the Lord. Lift up your hands to him for the lives of your children, who faint from hunger at the head of every street" (Lamentations 2:19).

"Give us today our daily bread" (Matthew 6:11).

"People were also bringing babies to Jesus to have him touch them. When the disciples saw this, they rebuked them. But Jesus called the children to him and said, 'Let the little children come to me, and do not hinder them, for the kingdom of God belongs to such as these' " (Luke 18: 15, 16).

"In the last days, God says, I will pour out my Spirit on all people. Your sons and your daughters will prophesy..." (Acts 2:17).

"As surely as you live, my lord, I am the woman who stood here beside you praying to the Lord. I prayed for this child, and the Lord has granted me what I asked of him. So now I give him to the Lord. For his whole life he will be given over to the Lord" (1 Samuel 1:25-28).

"He took a little child and had him stand among them. Taking him in his arms, he said to them, 'Whoever welcomes one of these little children in my name welcomes me; and whoever welcomes me does not welcome me but the one who sent me' " (Mark 9:36, 37).

"To Timothy, my dear son: ...I thank God, whom I serve, as my forefathers did, with a clear conscience, as night and day I constantly remember you in my prayers. Recalling your tears, I long to see you, ...I have been reminded of your sincere faith, which first lived in your grandmother Lois and in your mother Eunice and, I am persuaded, now lives in you also. For this reason I remind you to fan into flame the gift of God, which is in you through the laying on of my hands. For God did not give us a spirit of timidity, but a spirit of power, of love and of self-discipline. So do not be ashamed to testify about our Lord..." (2 Timothy 1:2-8).

"See I will send you the prophet Elijah, before that great and dreadful day of the Lord comes. He will turn the hearts of the fathers to their children, and the hearts of the children to their fathers; or else I will come and strike the land with a curse" (Malachi 4:5,6).

"From the lips of children and infants you have ordained praise because of your enemies, to silence the foe and the avenger" (Psalm 8:2).

Second Prayer Watch: 9 p.m.

Theme: Spiritual Preparation

Prayer Guide:

1. Personal prayer with Christ for spiritual preparation and strengthening against the flesh and the enemy (to submit your will to God and not to the flesh or the devil).

2. Pray that pastors and leaders will have spiritual strength and discernment. Pray that they will not fall into the traps of the enemy (to destroy their ministry and testimony through sexual immorality, financial dishonesty, disunity in leadership).

3. Pray for the congregation to stand firm in testing and trials (confronting and dealing with the enemy's attempts to weaken the church through gossip, dissension and division).

Scripture:

" 'Be always on the watch, and pray that you may be able to escape all that is about to happen, and that you may be able to stand before the Son of Man.' Each day Jesus was teaching at the temple, and each evening he went out to spend the night on the hill called the Mount of Olives" (Luke 21:36,37).

"Then he returned to his disciples and found them sleeping. 'Could you men not keep watch with me for one hour?' he asked Peter. 'Watch and pray so that you will not fall into temptation. The spirit is willing, but the body is weak'" (Matthew 26:40, 41).

"For the sinful nature desires what is contrary to the Spirit,

and the Spirit what is contrary to the sinful nature. They are in conflict with each other so that you do not do what you want…The acts of the sinful nature are obvious: sexual immorality, impurity… hatred, discord, jealousy, fits of rage, selfish ambition, dissensions, factions and envy… and the like" (Galatians 5:17-21).

"Because he himself suffered when he was tempted, he is able to help those who are being tempted"(Hebrews 2:18).

"Therefore he is able to save completely those who come to God through him, because he always lives to intercede for them" (Hebrews 7:25).

"His divine power has given us everything we need for life and godliness through our knowledge of him who called us by his own glory and goodness. Through these he has given us his very great and precious promises, so that through them you may participate in the divine nature and escape the corruption in the world caused by evil desires" (2 Peter 1: 3,4).

"And lead us not into temptation, but deliver us from the evil one" (Matthew 6:13).

"For though we live in the world, we do not wage war as the world does. The weapons we fight with are not the weapons of the world. On the contrary, they have divine power to demolish strongholds. We demolish arguments and every pretension that sets itself up against the knowledge of God, and we take captive every thought to make it obedient to Christ" (2 Corinthians 10:3-5).

"For this reason, since the day we heard about you, we have not stopped praying for you and asking God to fill

you with the knowledge of his will through all spiritual wisdom and understanding. And we pray this in order that you may live a life worthy of the Lord and may please him in every way: bearing fruit in every good work, growing in the knowledge of God, being strengthened with all power according to his glorious might so that you may have great endurance and patience, and joyfully giving thanks to the Father, who has qualified you to share in the inheritance of the saints in the kingdom of light" (Colossians 1:9-12).

Third Prayer Watch: 12 Midnight

Theme: Spiritual Battle

Prayer Guide:

1. Pray that we, like Peter, would learn from our previous failures, and return to the spiritual battle prepared to stand firm in Christ and to help others to stand firm.

2. Pray that the church would learn once again to pray using the Word, declaring and obeying truth to overcome the lies and deception of the enemy.

3. Pray for persecuted Christians around the world that they may stand firm in Christ, even to the point of death.

Scripture:

"It will be good for those servants whose master finds them watching when he comes. I tell you the truth, he will dress himself to serve, will have them recline at the table and will come and wait on them. It will be good for those servants whose master finds them ready, even if he comes in the second or third watch of the night" (Luke 12:37,38).

"Simon, Simon, Satan has asked to sift you as wheat. But I have prayed for you, Simon, that your faith may not fail. And when you have turned back, strengthen your brothers" (Luke 22:31,32).

"About midnight Paul and Silas were praying and singing hymns to God, and the other prisoners were listening to them. Suddenly there was such a violent earthquake that

the foundations of the prison were shaken. At once all the prison doors flew open, and everybody's chains came loose…The jailer called for lights, rushed in and fell trembling before Paul and Silas. He then brought them out and asked, 'Sirs, what must I do to be saved?" (Acts 16:25-26, 29-30).

"Finally, be strong in the Lord and in his mighty power. Put on the full armor of God so that you can take your stand against the devil's schemes. For our struggle is not against flesh and blood, but against the rulers, against the authorities, against the powers of this dark world and against the spiritual forces of evil in the heavenly realms. Therefore put on the full armor of God, so that when the day of evil comes, you may be able to stand your ground, and after you have done everything, to stand" (Ephesians 6: 10 – 13).

"Stand firm then, with the belt of truth buckled around your waist, with the breastplate of righteousness in place, and with your feet fitted with the readiness that comes from the gospel of peace. In addition to all this, take up the shield of faith, with which you can extinguish all the flaming arrows of the evil one. <u>Take the helmet of salvation and the sword of the Spirit, which is the word of God. And pray in the Spirit on all occasions with all kinds of prayers and requests. With this in mind, be alert and always keep on praying for all the saints</u>" (Ephesians 6: 14 – 18).

"For the word of God is living and active. Sharper than any double-edged sword, it penetrates even to dividing soul and spirit, joints and marrow; it judges the thoughts and attitudes of the heart" (Hebrews 4:12).

"You, dear children, are from God and have overcome them, because the one who is in you is greater than the

one who is in the world" (1 John 4:4).

"In this you greatly rejoice, though now for a little while you may have had to suffer grief in all kinds of trials. These have come so that your faith – of greater worth than gold, which perishes even though refined by fire – may be proved genuine and may result in praise, glory and honor when Jesus Christ is revealed" (1 Peter 1:6-7).

"Then the dragon was enraged at the woman and went off to make war against the rest of her offspring – those who obey God's commandments and hold to the testimony of Jesus" (Revelation 12:17).

"When he opened the fifth seal, I saw under the altar the souls of those who had been slain because of the word of God and the testimony they had maintained. They called out in loud voices, 'How long, Sovereign Lord, holy and true, until you judge the inhabitants of the earth and avenge our blood?' Then each of them was given a white robe, and they were told to wait a little longer, until the number of their fellow servants and brothers who were to be killed as they had been was completed" (Revelation 6:9-11).

"The God of peace will soon crush Satan under your feet" (Romans 16:20).

"Now have come the salvation and the power and the kingdom of our God, and the authority of his Christ. For the accuser of our brothers, who accuses them before our God day and night, has been hurled down. They overcame him by the blood of the Lamb and by the word of their testimony; they did not love their lives so much as to shrink from death" (Revelation 12:10, 11).

"I saw heaven standing open and there before me was a white horse, whose rider is called Faithful and True. With justice he judges and makes war. His eyes are like blazing fire, and on his head are many crowns. He has a name written on him that no one knows but he himself. He is dressed in a robe dipped in blood, and <u>his name is the Word of God.</u> The armies of heaven were following him, riding on white horses and dressed in fine linen, white and clean. <u>Out of his mouth comes a sharp sword with which to strike down the nations"</u> (Revelation 19:11 – 15).

" 'Not by might nor by power, but by my Spirit,' says the Lord Almighty" (Zechariah 4:6).

Fourth Prayer Watch: 3 a.m.

Theme: Christ's Kingdom

Prayer Guide:

1. Pray for a mighty spiritual movement in your church and city as believers from all denominations unite to join upraised hands in intercession before the throne of God.

2. Pray for an in-breaking of Christ's kingdom in your church and community through repentance, revival and community transformation.

3. Pray for Christ's return when he will establish forever his kingdom on the earth and bring an end to Satan´s influence – Maranatha!

Scripture:

"Very early in the morning, while it was still dark, Jesus got up, left the house and went off to a solitary place, where he prayed" (Mark 1: 35).

"During the fourth watch of the night Jesus went out to them, walking on the lake. When the disciples saw him walking on the lake, they were terrified. 'It's a ghost,' they said, and cried out in fear. But Jesus immediately said to them: 'Take courage! It is I. Don't be afraid.' 'Lord, if it's you,' Peter replied, 'tell me to come to you on the water.' 'Come,' he said" (Matthew 14: 25 -29).

"Therefore keep watch because you do not know when the owner of the house will come back – whether in the evening, or at midnight, or when the rooster crows, or at dawn. If he comes suddenly, do not let him find you sleep-

ing. What I say to you, I say to everyone: 'Watch!' " (Mark 13:35 -37).

"During the last watch of the night the Lord looked down from the pillar of fire and cloud at the Egyptian army and threw it into confusion. He made the wheels of their chariots come off so that they had difficulty driving. And the Egyptians said, 'Let's get away from the Israelites! The Lord is fighting for them against Egypt' " (Exodus 14:24 -25).

"Then the Lord said to Moses, 'Stretch out your hand over the sea so that the waters may flow back over the Egyptians and their chariots and horsemen.' Moses stretched out his hand over the sea, and at daybreak the sea went back to its place. ...The water flowed back and covered the chariots and horsemen – the entire army of Pharaoh that had followed the Israelites into the sea. Not one of them survived" (Exodus 14:26-28).

"As long as Moses held up his hands, the Israelites were winning, but whenever he lowered his hands, the Amalekites were winning. When Moses' hands grew tired, they took a stone and put it under him and he sat on it. Aaron and Hur held his hands up – one on one side, one on the other – so that his hands remained steady till sunset. So Joshua overcame the Amalekite army with the sword. Then the Lord said to Moses, 'Write this on a scroll as something to be remembered and make sure that Joshua hears it, because I will completely blot out the memory of Amalek from under heaven.' Moses built an altar and called it The Lord is my Banner. He said: 'For hands were lifted up to the throne of the Lord. The Lord will be at war against the Amalekites from generation to generation' "(Exodus 17:11-16).

"I want men everywhere to lift up holy hands in prayer,

without anger or disputing" (1 Timothy 2:8).

"Early on the first day of the week, while it was still dark, Mary Magdalene went to the tomb and saw that the stone had been removed from the entrance"(John 20:1).

"They found the stone rolled away from the tomb, but when they entered, they did not find the body of the Lord Jesus. While they were wondering about this, suddenly two men in clothes that gleamed like lightning stood be side them. In their fright the women bowed down with their faces to the ground, but the men said to them, 'Why do you look for the living among the dead? He is not here; he has risen!' " (Luke 24:2-5).

"And if the Spirit of him who raised Jesus from the dead is living in you, he who raised Christ from the dead will also give life to your mortal bodies through his Spirit, who lives in you" (Romans 8:11).

"Come, Lord Jesus!" (Revelation 22:20).

"Your kingdom come, your will be done on earth as it is in heaven" (Matthew 6:10).

"After the Lord Jesus had spoken to them, he was taken up into heaven and he sat at the right hand of God. Then the disciples went out and preached everywhere, and the Lord worked with them and confirmed his word by the signs that accompanied it" (Mark 16:19,20).

"The kingdom of the world has become the kingdom of our Lord and Christ, and he will reign forever and ever" (Revelation 11:15).

THE DIVINE PRAYER CLOCK SCHEDULE

6 a.m. – Morning Hour of Incense (God´s People)

9 a.m. – Third Hour of Prayer (Anointing of the Holy Spirit)

12 noon – Sixth Hour of Prayer (The Nations)

3 p.m. – Ninth Hour of Prayer (The Throne of Grace)

6 p.m. – First Prayer Watch (The Children)

9 p.m. – Second Prayer Watch (Spiritual Preparation)

12 midnight – Third Prayer Watch (Spiritual Battle)

3 a.m. – Fourth Prayer Watch (Christ's Kingdom)

Day Prayers
12
9
3
6

Night Prayers
12
9
3
6